When A Man Of God Hurts You

Overcoming a Painful Relationship with a Man in Ministry

Author Merilyn Renee Williams

Copyright © 2010 by **Merilyn Renee Williams**

This book is a work of fiction based on a true story. Names, characters and locations have been changed.

All rights reserved. Except as permitted under the U.S. Copyright Act of 1976, no part of this publication may be reproduced, distributed, or transmitted in any form or by any means, or stored in a database or retrieval system, without the prior written permission of the publisher.

If you have purchased this book with a "dull" or "missing" cover, you may have purchased an unauthorized or stolen book. Please immediately contact the publisher advising where, when, and how you purchased the book.

Editor: Carla M. Dean, *U Can Mark My Word*
Book Cover Designer: Eduardo Lopez
Typesetting: Carla M. Dean, *U Can Mark My Word*

Printed in the United States of America

First Edition

DEDICATION

This is dedicated to the emotions of hurt, pain, sorrow, and the scars they leave on the hearts and minds of women.

To the many women who have been hurt, when all they wanted was love.

To the women who are still holding on to hurt and resentment.

To the women who need the power to overcome.

This is dedicated to you!

ACKNOWLEDGEMENTS

Each book written is really the product of many people, because all those who touch the life of an author influence his or her work. First and foremost, I certainly thank my father God. An acknowledgment in this book will never measure up to what God has been in my life, but it is to him that I give all praise to.

Big thanks to my daughters Zuri & Jehlani, just for being my gems. Very special thanks to my parents Deacon Ben & Elder Florine Williams for being there through my ups and downs, in between, and unexplainable times. It is one thing to give birth to a child and raise it, but when you choose to raise another person's child, that speaks volumes and is honorable. For I am a CHOSEN child, and they are certainly my heroes! To my uncle and teacher, Bishop Victor D. Agee, a mighty man of God who has imparted so much into my life. Words will never be able to thank him enough for the person he has been to me. My Pastor James Brooks Jr., before he became my pastor he was always there for me to encourage & uplift me. Always taking the time out of his busy schedule just for me, I am truly thankful for him. The memory of my biological mother, Marsha Faye Williams, a lot of her rests within me. Thanks to my siblings, Rosalie, Brashawn, Michelle, Lawrence, Melvin, Mark, Patrick, Antoine, and the memory of my oldest brother, Kevin.

I also would like to thank my ENTIRE family and friends who have stood behind me and continuously pushed me forward. Through all trials and happy times, we are still family, and that will never change. I am thankful for every one of you.

~SPECIAL THANK YOU~

There are many people who were closely involved through the reasoning for this book. Many have prayed for me, taken me to lunch and listened to me while I vented, been a shoulder to cry on, chatted with me via the internet, phone calls, text messages, Facebook, or whatever else they have done. I am truly thankful and eternally grateful for each of them, and they deserve recognition of their own. So, I give a special thanks to the following:

Harmony Community Church, Praise Temple Of Restoration, New Greater Exodus M.B. Church, Work Of His Hands Ministries, Christian Sisters Connection, Women Empowering Women, Christian Greater Rock, Shaneka Sims, Danielle Moore, Sadie Tigner, Buffy Jackson, Victoria Hester, Erica Burnside, Tamara Lee, Tamika Payton, and all of the ladies of Westinghouse Warriors Class of 1996, Nakia Stanley, Philip Robinson, Shanina McCregg, Arthur Wood, Dekendrick Dix, Pastor Tim Smith, Pastor T A Fountain, My life coach Dr. Walter Sims, Latrecha Sandifer, Carolyn Coleman, Author Terrence Ellery, Antoinette Coleman, Angie Whitehead, Corey Barrow, Dennis Williams, Linda Stanley, Audrey Bickerstaff, Bernadine Sandifer, Adrion Harris, Sandra Ayala, Shana Stanton, Lillian Brown, Dean Tate, Minister Lisa Cannon, Jerrold Norwood, Pastors Tracey & Frank Brim, Nikki Twiggs, David Johnson, Aisha Keys, Rakiah Polk, Marvella Williams, Sharron Hawkins, Attorney Geannetta Jackson, Bishop D. Jerome Watson, Kevin Murphy, Prophet Faye Watkins, Myriah Robinson, Myrisah Robinson, Elder Durand Howard, Daniel Aguilar, Pastor Ron Thomas and Overseer Derrick Coleman.

Sincere thanks to all of you for being there for me in any way that you were. I am very appreciative for every single ministry, relative, and friend listed.

When A Man

Of God

Hurts You

Overcoming a Painful Relationship with a Man in Ministry

Introduction

*Everything that begins beautiful doesn't end beautiful.
If it did, things would never end.*

When a Man of God Hurts You is designed to help women overcome hurt they may have experienced from relationships with men in ministry. Not just the deacon, usher, or armor bearer, but the elders, pastors, bishops, and apostles. For some reason, we as women often think if a man is leading a ministry, the relationship will be better…or in fact, last. Truly, many have thought that way and still do. Even though it's just a title, there is still a man underneath that title. Yet, he is a man of God. If he wears that cloth, you would certainly think they would behave differently from the worldly gentlemen we meet.

Now, by no means are we judging all men of God. There are plenty of awesome men of God who live the life they preach and teach about. This is just a story of an experience a young lady went through with ONE man of God and how she overcame it. I am sure she is not the only woman who has been hurt by an elder in the Lord's church. This book is not to bash the men of the cloth, but it's about overcoming, which is what she did. No matter how hurt she was and what the man did to her, she overcame…and YOU can, too. Let her story encourage you!

Sometimes women ignore red flags, give too much too soon, and let their guard completely down before analyzing what's really before them. After reading this book, women should be able to recognize the red flags, and women should feel empowered and encouraged to love again.

When a Man of God Hurts You tells about a relationship that began as a fairytale and ended up a painful nightmare. Yet, it doesn't end there. It was the worst pain ever. Still, after being depressed, crying for weeks, etc., she OVERCAME! The author wants you to release the pain and truly forgive. If you learned from it, then truly it was worth it. Please know total forgiveness is essential. Sometimes you have to thank God for the mayhem in your life. It reveals the true character of people and the strength you possess to overcome opposition and demonic forces. If God brought you to it, he will surely bring you through it.

Chapter 1: Personal Experience

You can close your eyes to things you don't want to see, but you cannot close your heart to things you don't want to feel.

One day after church, my uncle called me into his office.

"Well, Facebook is getting folks in trouble lately, huh, Gwen?" he said, then sat down at his desk and logged into his Facebook page.

My cousin Cee-Cee was in his office with me, and we were both sitting there with blank looks on our faces, thinking, *What is he talking about?*

My uncle went to his inbox to retrieve a message that a bishop, who had been my friend for quite a while and who I've done work for, had sent to him. In the message, he asked my uncle how he felt about my spiritual walk and did he think I would be a good First Lady. He told my uncle that friendship and love was not enough when choosing a mate. Therefore, he wanted to know more about me.

I just sat there thinking, *WOW! Why didn't he discuss all this with me first? He knew my phone number, address, email, instant messenger, and every other means of contacting me. Why did he go to my uncle?* That puzzled me. I was almost in tears reading his email.

Then Aunt Bernadette walked in and joined the discussion, while I was still in shock. Cee-Cee asked me if I knew he liked me to that extent, to which I replied, "I knew he liked me somewhat, but dang, why did he have to tell my uncle first?"

I told Aunt Bernadette that for the last few months, the only men who approached me were men of clergy. That's when she expressed to me that I have the look that men of clergy seek in a woman: tall, thin, and with long weave down my back. In my mind, I was upset about the fact that me looking like a Barbie doll is what attracted men of clergy to me. In fact, there was more to me than just my outer beauty.

My uncle then asked me had Bishop and I ever kissed or anything. I told him we had lunch and even rode in the same vehicle, but that he had never made a move to kiss me. Bishop had been very respectful of my mind, body, and soul. Plus, we were just friends. I informed my uncle that when I first met Bishop, I was working for him. I made the ordination certificates, did videotaping, and took pictures when he ordained five evangelists. We had just been friends ever since then. In fact, when I first met him, I thought he was the most arrogant, pompous jerk I had ever come in contact with. However, since I was doing a job, I looked past it. Once I got to know him as a friend, he still had a huge ego, but I dealt with it. Finding out he liked me as more than a friend was a shock, and I couldn't wait to get home to call him.

My uncle let him know through a short message that he wouldn't respond via the internet, and that if he really wanted to discuss me, he was more than welcome to come to the church and meet with him. Bishop responded to my uncle but did not agree to meet with him. When I spoke to Bishop that evening about it, he told me that he was doing a background check on me. Being a bishop, he believed he didn't have time to waste dating when choosing a wife.

Bishop and I would always chat via Yahoo messenger. Both of our laptops were equipped with webcams, so he introduced me to Skype, the real-time video and voice chat that enabled him to see and hear whatever I was doing, and vice versa.

Whenever we would video chat, he always sat in one spot on the end of his couch. After getting off work and getting the kids settled down, I would climb into my bed and video call him. This became a nightly ritual for us. We spent our evenings debriefing about our days, then picked up our bibles and studied the word of God.

Bishop was strictly a King James Version reader, while I preferred the New International Version. He would fuss at me every night for reading from the NIV. He would teach me about all kinds of things. Now, I'm a girl who has been in church all my life, but the way he taught the same familiar scriptures I had been taught gave a whole different theory on them. The way he broke the scriptures down made sense, but where he got his theories from I couldn't tell you. I didn't debate with him, though, since he was more of bible reader than I was.

When I would express to him how I felt he was manipulating the scriptures and making them conducive to his likeness, he would get upset, telling me that he had been to seminary and all. So, I would just leave it alone. We would go on and on about ministry, the word of God, and then pray together. One night, I led the prayer, and when I finished he told me, "Girl, that's sexy. I didn't know you could bombard heaven like that. I think I'm in love." Keep in mind he could see me while I was praying. We normally ended our chat about 3:00 a.m.

One afternoon, after we had started dating, Sugar Lump, as I referred to Bishop, called me, and being the natural storyteller he was, he began telling me about statuses. According to him, the status you are in a person's life determines what level of affection and access you are granted with that individual. In politics, the alderman has access to his ward; the mayor has access to the city; and the president…well, you know he has access to it all. In relationships, there are four statuses. Affection and access should be appropriate to the level of the status you're on.

- Friend—this relationship involves chatting via phone, over the internet, and spending occasional time together in person. There is no intimacy beyond a hug. At this stage, you are learning a person.
- Girlfriend—there is a little intimacy involved, maybe some kissing. No other person should have the access of calling at any hour and escorting her to events, engagements, outings, etc. This is the first stage of commitment. Dating others is out of the question.
- Fiancé—level of affection is still about the same here. Just entering the zone of taking on his name and combining families and incomes soon. At this level, you should know all there is to know about your soon-to-be life partner. There should be no surprises from here on out.

- Wife—like the president, all access granted! You take on his last name, and both have equal rights to property. The level of affection here is all in. The bed of marriage is undefiled. The wife has a right to her husband's body, just as he has a right to hers.

While listening to him, I sat on my couch wondering what the point of his long tale was. Sugar Lump then began telling me that he had been friends with and dated many women, with a lot of them not having passed the friend status.

"I don't feel they were intelligent enough or understood the mantle on my life, but you're different," Sugar Lump told me. "You've been an awesome friend to me since day one, and you really understand ministry. I think you're ready to go further with me. I already love you. So, my next question is, will you be my girlfriend? All the other men who want you can't have the access to you that I have if you accept being my girlfriend. Men of God don't need three to five years to decide if a person should be their wife. We know between six months to a year if she is suitable enough to be a wife. You're well on your way. So, will you be my girlfriend?"

My first thought was the titles "boyfriend" and "girlfriend" sounded juvenile for a thirty-year-old woman and a forty-two-year-old man. But, my answer was yes.

After we hung up, I started thinking back to the discussion I had in my uncle's office when my cousin and aunt were present. My thoughts were all over the place. I knew he wanted more. My concern was if I could handle what was before me. He wasn't like anyone I had ever dated. He wasn't average. He was one of the ones God had chosen to be a voice to his people.

I began to second guess myself for a minute, but then remembered the words of my uncle Vincent. *You can be a pastor's wife, the First Lady of a church. Don't ever minimize what God is trying to maximize, including you. Don't downgrade yourself. In fact, one of your cousins is a First Lady and her life took a full turn becoming a pastor's wife, but it's working for her. So, hear me when I tell you that.*

So, I began attempting my transformation mentally in preparation for what was before me. I stopped looking at the surface of things in life and looked at everything deeper. Life is more than what you can see with your natural eyes.

Aunt Bernadette was one of my aunts whom I looked up to. So, I emailed her about becoming a woman of grace, class, style, and sophistication. I felt I needed to drop my vintage t-shirts and red, black, and green headbands in order to become more ladylike. I had no problem meeting men. However, this man was different. Even though he loved my vibrant personality, I knew from the hints he dropped there were some things about me that needed to change. So, with Aunt Bernadette knowing my personality, including how I dressed and talked, she would be the one to coach me. I simply asked for her assistance with a makeover from the inside out.

Her emailed response was not necessarily one that I cared to read, though. She replied, *Gwendolyn, when someone loves you, they love you for who you are, not who you become. Whatever attracted him to you in the first place should be enough to keep him. Your family knows you're silly, free-hearted, helpful, and at times wishy washy. Why change who you are for another person? That's not love.*

As I sat reading her email, I found myself mad at this lady. I felt she didn't understand what I needed from her. It caused me to cry for a while. I had a massive headache and kept thinking no one would understand what was happening to me, and I really needed them to. *Why didn't she understand?* was all I kept thinking while crying. I soon shook it off and knew I had to take matters into my own hands.

Bishop was quite an arrogant man. It was hard telling him anything, but that was my crazy little man and I was crazy about him.

One week, I got sick with the flu and was glued to the couch for days. When Bishop called to see how I was doing, I let him know I was sick as ever and didn't have the energy to go out and get medicine. So, he came by my place maybe an hour later with some medicine, juice, and the first card he had ever given me…a get-well card. My oldest daughter went out to his car and got the things from him. After getting the items, I called to thank him for being sweet.

"You'll be a great husband, I'm sure," I told him.

He replied, "When I was married, I was a good husband…the best, in fact." (There was his arrogance coming out.)

"Well, honey," I said, "tell me why your marriage ended after eighteen years."

"She began to question me and lacked trust in me a while after I had began pastoring," he responded. "I don't like arguing or not being trusted, and no woman is going to question me. I provide and rule in my home."

I asked, "Well, did you give her reason to question you and not trust you?"

"She became insecure," was his reply, "because my days were long, and I was away from home more than I was there. My members would call me at whatever hour, and sometimes I would have to leave to go handle things in the middle of the night. She had been the perfect wife for eighteen years and gave me my youngest son. But, she was just average. She didn't think deeper, dressed plain, and did not understand ministry at all. In fact, she told my mother that I married her, not a church. She was not in agreement with me becoming a pastor. So, after eighteen years, the friction began."

I then asked, "What happened with the first wife?"

"I was young and she got pregnant, so I married her. She gave me two sons, but it was just a mistake I made. We were both young and immature."

After listening to him telling me about two wives and being single for about eight years now, I asked him if he was ready to marry again. He responded by saying yes and then expressed his desire to marry someone who understood and complemented him in ministry.

I helped him a lot with his ministry, which was small and that he had been pastoring for about twelve or thirteen years. He had asked me to assist his media ministry by showing them what I did for my church so they could begin working on his media ministry. So, I hooked up with two of his members, one being an evangelist whom he had ordained. Ariel was a fireball for God from the day I met her. The other sister, Cassandra, was Hispanic. She was very sweet, quiet, and had a very humble spirit. We all connected instantly. I loved those ladies. We worked well together and became the greatest of friends. The ladies started coming to my place, and we would work on media stuff, have refreshments, and talk. I showed them some of the things I did as far as creating DVDs and so forth. They talked about their pastor and how awesome he was, while I just smiled on the inside.

At this time, they didn't know we were seeing each other, but I was a familiar face to them in the church. I would come sometimes and record his service. I would take a seat and say amen here & there, and when he gave the benediction, I would greet a few folks and then quietly exit. He would always call me later and repeat the whole sermon as if I didn't hear it. I knew preaching and teaching was a passion for him, so I just listened all over again as he spoke with excitement in his voice. At this time of the night, we would be on Skype. I'd be in my bed, he'd be planted on his couch, and we would just smile at each other. I always let him know what an awesome job he did on his sermon and how great he looked. He was a sharp dresser, all the way down to his shoes.

My Sugar Lump was a handful when he wanted to be. We would end our nights with an "I love you" and kisses to our computer screens. Yeah, we were a corny pair…yet, in love.

During one period while we were dating, my car broke down and the whole engine had to be replaced. I was without a car for a while, so Bishop would take the girls to school most mornings and drop me off at work. While with him, my daughters took the opportunity to question him, or should I say, call themselves telling on me when I would discipline them. I guess they felt that since he was a pastor, he would tell their mama to take it easy on them. Needless to say, it sure didn't work.

Sometimes, if we got up and out early enough, we would stop and get some breakfast before he took me to work. One morning, I had on some jeans that were truly snug around my butt. At this time, I was about a size ten, so my butt looked nice in a pair of jeans to the male eye. As I was exiting his Benz, he grabbed my butt and said, "Now that's a nice ass." At this point, we had never even really kissed, yet here he was booty grabbing.

"What was that about?" I asked him, shocked by the great bishop's actions and potty mouth.

"I couldn't resist," he replied. "Those jeans look great on you."

I just smiled, kissed him on his forehead, and entered my job.

Later that evening when I got home, my cell phone was acting retarded. So, he brought over one of his old cell phones for me to switch my number over since we had the same phone company. While sitting in the car with him and programming his phone to my number, I decided to ask him about the whole status thing.

"Baby, now you were booty grabbing this morning and everything. Is that the appropriate level of affection for the status we're on? Do boyfriend and girlfriend grab body parts?"

He responded by saying, "I was in my flesh and shouldn't have done that. On our level, it should be hugs, kisses, and holding hands. That's about it."

Then he turned off the light in his car, held my hand, pulled me close to him, and began to give me a *real* kiss. He was gentle as his lips pressed against mine. Our lips slowly parted as the moistness of our tongues met one another. I took his cheek in my hand, caressing his masculine face as he continued to kiss me slowly and passionately. Then his hands began to roam, and he rubbed them across my breasts and back. I grabbed his hand and held it in my hand. We slowly pulled away from each other and then embraced one another tightly.

He looked into my eyes. "Gwendolyn, I love you, and I dream of the day I can have access to all of you."

After telling him I loved him, too, I went back inside my apartment before things had the chance to go any further.

I had butterflies in my stomach like a teenager. I thought to myself, *I haven't felt like this in a long time. I hope this brother isn't a disappointment. Then again, he's a man of God, and I am so ready for something real. I don't want to date anyone who is not saved and under a covering at this point in my life anyway.*

He returned to his home, and later that evening, we jumped on Skype, had our bible study, and conducted our nightly ritual as usual.

One afternoon, while on a field trip with my oldest daughter, I decided the next day I would spend the afternoon with my Sugar Lump. So, I called my cousins, Nina and Kia, and my friends from his church to get an idea as to what he liked so I could plan a nice little afternoon rendezvous.

He had expressed to me that the women in his past showed him how much they loved him by the things they did for him. When he told me that he hadn't seen me give anything to him and do for him to show my love, at first, I thought to myself, *He has never given me anything but medicine, a get-well card, and occasionally paid for dinner.* Then, I thought, *Okay, Gwendolyn, he's a man of God. So, more is required of me.*

Bishop explained to me numerous times that being in a relationship with a pastor is hard work. Therefore, I needed to step my game up. After texting and talking to my girls about ideas for the date, I gathered some things after the field trip for my afternoon rendezvous.

The next morning, I got the girls up and off to school. As I was returning home, I stopped at Dunkin Donuts and got my Sugar Lump his coffee just the way he liked it. Arriving at his apartment, I called him to come out and get it. After he approached my car, I handed him the coffee and an invitation to join me that afternoon for a date in my apartment.

After leaving there, I returned home to make sure my place was spotless. I made a cheese and cracker tray, which I placed on the table in my living room. I sat out some juice and water, and even lit some candles. When my Sugar Lump arrived, I greeted him with open arms and a kiss.

Bishop had been in my apartment many times before, and he would always just take a seat in the living room. This time, however, he decided to come in and walk around. He looked in every room, including the kitchen. He looked at the stove, in the refrigerator, and around the sink. He even looked in the girls' room and commented on them having too much, saying he didn't have all that when he was a child. Next, he went in the bathroom to look under the sink, in the medicine cabinet, and everywhere else. He laughed at my supply of body wash and tampons.

"Geesh! How much hygiene and personal care items does

one woman need?" he said.

By now, I was just looking at him, not believing he was seriously inspecting my apartment this hard. He then went in my bedroom and sat on my bed.

"This is a very high bed, and it's quite comfortable. It's even bigger than my bed," he told me.

He opened some of my dresser drawers, peeked inside, and closed them back. He noticed I kept a picture of him on my dresser. Then he went to my huge walk-in closet. After looking at my shoe collection and clothing for a few moments, he had me go get a chair so he could sit down in front of my closet and pick out the shoes I couldn't wear while dating him. He picked out flip-flops, shoes with heels above three inches, and any that were animal prints. He also went through my clothes and told me no shirts that were sleeveless, had spaghetti straps, and didn't require a bra. Skirts above the knee and any slacks that showed off my figure were definitely out of the question. The whole time I was sitting on my bed thinking, *Are you serious?*

"You're with me now," he said. "So, you're a reflection of me. You're going to be a pastor's wife and the First Lady of a church. You have a tattoo on your arm that needs not to be seen at all. Whether you're with me or not, folks know who you belong to."

"So what's the big deal about my shoes?" I asked him.

"Were you not listening to me? You cannot wear these little vintage t-shirts and flip-flops or hooker heels. I won't allow it."

I tried not to look upset. Instead, I just sat there quietly.

He found a dress I had worn to my uncle and aunt's birthday party. It was a sexy, yet classy little black dress. He saw the pictures of me in the dress on Facebook, and I think the attention I got from other men was what made him not like the dress. He took the dress off the hanger, folded it up, and returned to the living room.

What the hell is he going to do with my dress? I was thinking.

We took a seat on the couch. He had brought his favorite movie for us to watch, *Willy Wonka & The Chocolate Factory*. That amazed me that it was his favorite movie. After popping in the DVD, I went to my room to get the bag I had for him. Once I handed it to him, he opened the bag to find it filled with scented candles, scented oils, and a card. He was all smiles.

I pressed play on the DVD player and sat close to him with my head on his chest, while we watched *Willy Wonka*. I listened to his heartbeat as I laid there wondering why he liked that movie so much. When the movie ended, I prepared a light lunch for us. However, before giving him his plate, I presented him with another gift. This second gift bag had a picture of me, a picture of me and him, a CD with love songs that made me think of him, and another card.

"Wow, Gwendolyn, you're showing me that you can step your game up, huh?"

I smiled and asked, "So is me giving you gifts the only way you know I love you?"

He started quoting the scripture. "For God so loved the world that he GAVE his only begotten son. Love gives, Gwendolyn. God gave his son for us to show each other love."

After eating our lunch, we started reading a psychology book to each other and a book about getting engaged, dealing with key questions we needed to ask each other. Some of the questions were deep. He asked me things about my past, the relationships with my children's fathers, my parents, and so forth. He even asked me how many sexual partners I've had. I answered most of his questions, even though I felt some were irrelevant.

When I asked him about his parents, he told me that he and his mother were close. Although she was a member of another church, she came to his church every Sunday when she left from attending service at her church home. He told me that he didn't have much of a relationship with his father. He wasn't a major part of his life. I knew he had married twice, had three sons, and been a business and property owner.

When I told him I knew about the children and asked why he never talked about them, he said he didn't have a relationship with any of them. The two oldest and him had fallen out many years ago, so they didn't talk. The youngest son was still a teenager, and they rarely spoke, as well. He didn't really explain to me the reasons why he didn't have relationships with the seeds he created. Then he told me since he had gotten his divorce, it was possible he had a six- or seven-year-old, but he wasn't certain because the young lady disappeared.

When I asked how many sexual partners he'd had, he replied, "You didn't answer me, but I'll answer you…373."

I almost passed out, until he laughed and told me that he was just kidding.

"It's been really about seventy-three women and three men."

Now he was getting a blank stare. "So you've tried same sex?" I asked.

"Yes, I was with a white man when I was younger and a few other men."

When I asked him if it was at his own freewill, he said yes, which caused me to raise a brow.

"Are you bi-sexual or what?" was my next question.

He kissed me and said, "Gwendolyn, all of that is behind me."

Without another word, I went into my room and returned with another gift. This bag contained a fifty-dollar gas card, a notebook, a pen engraved with his name, as well as another card. All the gift bags were black with white lettering. One said *Faith*, another *Hope*, and of course, the other said *Love*.

He hugged and squeezed me so tight. While we were standing pelvis to pelvis, I thought to myself, *He's going to get an erection if he doesn't let go of me.*

He sat down on the couch, and I sat on the floor in between his legs. I massaged his legs and thighs, rubbed his hands, and caressed his face. Then I got on my knees in front of him and kissed him. He pulled me up off my knees and placed me in a position where I was straddling him. With our genitals pressed together, we kissed passionately. My heart was beating fast, and my body parts were getting extremely moist.

He gently had me lay on my back on the couch and climbed on top of me. I was thinking, *I know he's not trying to go there.* He was on top of me for the longest, continually kissing me and grinding his pelvic area into mine. Then it dawned on me that he was doing all this without an erection. *Dang, he has some serious self-control.* I, on the other hand, was extremely hot, bothered, and my panties were beyond wet. Finally, he came up for air and began gathering his things so he could return home. Before leaving, he kissed me on my forehead and proceeded to go home.

When he left, I was still wondering how he could do that much kissing, rubbing, touching, and grinding without an erection. My thoughts were all over the place.

Bishop and I would always talk about ministry. I had been raised in church all my life. I also had the opportunity to work somewhat closely with my uncle Vincent, whom is also a pastor. I knew a little something about the ins and outs of ministry. So, he would tell me his vision, and wherever I could help him in ministry, I did.

Working in ministry is a passion of mine, and I think that's one of things that attracted Bishop to me. I created flyers, pluggers, did door-to-door evangelizing with him, and if members needed a ride, I would pick them up and drop them off. I even stayed up all night once pulling video footage of his sermons so he could be aired on a cable access network. I stayed up literally twenty-four hours straight trying to help his vision come to pass.

One day, my mother said to me, "Gwendolyn, I know you love this man and that you all are talking marriage, but I see you doing all the giving. What does he do for you? Besides him seeing your kids in his church, does he even have a strong relationship with them? Gwendolyn, I think he's using you. Open up those pretty brown eyes and pay attention."

Instead of taking heed to my mother's words, I got mad at her and continued doing what I was doing. Whatever he needed me to do, I did it. I loved him, and there was just simply nothing I wouldn't do for him. Every month when I went grocery shopping, he would give me his grocery list. So, as I was shopping for my house, I shopped for his, too.

One afternoon, we were chatting via Yahoo and he told me that his cell phone was off. Since he didn't have the money to pay it, I paid the bill for him. It would be a bit embarrassing for the pastor's cell phone to be off, right? That was one of the first bills I assisted him with. Next, I helped with his lights, cable, and rent.

"Sugar Lump, how did you manage all these years without a secular job?" I asked him one day.

He replied by saying he had more members before he dated me, and therefore, he was doing better. Then he blamed me for his members leaving. He said his friend Sharon helped him a lot, but when she left his church after finding out he was dating me, all of that ended. Many of the members were her relatives or friends of hers. So, when she walked, they walked. However, as told to me by some of his remaining members, they were also upset with him because she had been in his life for over six years and he had taken extreme advantage of her. They added that he had led her on by making her think she would one day be his wife. Needless to say, she was hurting. As a result, he was left with about fifteen members.

He told me, "You're going to be a bishop's wife, so act accordingly. When you marry a full-time pastor, a lot will rest in your lap. Have you taken notice that a lot of pastors' wives are well educated and have excellent paying jobs? They know love offerings or salary can change, so they have to carry the weight of the household. So, what you do for me, you're supposed to."

While he was speaking, I kept thinking to myself, *Okay, he keeps saying wife, but I'm just a girlfriend. I can't maintain two households. If I could, I would pay all of my parents' bills. How am I going to pull this off?*

Then he said that he loved me and expressed his need for me to help him. So, instead of maintaining my needs, I helped maintain his. Besides, I felt like I was sowing on good ground since he was going to be my husband.

One evening, Bishop called and told me that we needed to pick out rings. So, we went online together to browse various websites, and we found nice rings for both of us. We even searched for honeymoon packages in nearby cities since you couldn't pay him to get on a plane. I teased him all the time about his fear of flying by saying, "What happened to God didn't give us the spirit of fear?"

So, we picked out rings, a honeymoon package, and even looked for neighborhoods to live in. He informed me that he would probably propose during church service on a Sunday, but he wouldn't tell me which week. Therefore, he suggested I be in attendance every Sunday. When I told him that I could possibly do that, with the exception of first Sundays and special services at my church, he got upset.

"You're preparing to be a wife," he had said. "If you're in your morning service, you don't need to be in your afternoon service. Come where your soon-to-be husband is and support me."

So, to keep an argument from happening, I made it a point to be at every one of his services.

My cousin Nina was getting married on a Sunday, and that same week, I let Bishop know.

"Baby, now this is my Nina getting married, and you know how I feel about her. So, I won't be in your service this Sunday."

His reply was, "Gwendolyn, I really need you this Sunday. It is imperative that you're there."

I didn't know how I would swing being at both churches

since I really needed to be there for my cousin. So, I stayed at her ceremony long enough to witness her kiss my new cousin-in-law. Then, I did ninety miles per hour leaving the church in order to get to Bishop's church. I even took my little brother with me. By the time I made it there, it was the middle of his service, and when it ended, he walked up to me with an attitude.

"Why did you bring Larry with you to church? I needed you here to take my members home because today is my mother's birthday and I'm taking her out," he said.

I was extremely heated and could have cursed him out real good! Here it is he had me leave my cousin's wedding just to drop people off, and then it was his mother's birthday and he didn't even tell me. Who in the hell does that in a relationship? Or as the young people say, where they do that at?

So, as calmly as possible, I replied, "Why didn't you state what you needed from me from the start, and you couldn't tell me it was your mother's birthday today?"

"Well, you see your cousins all the time, and my mama doesn't like you. So, there was no need to tell you it was her birthday."

I took a deep breath before responding. I already knew his mother didn't like me because she felt I was too young for her son. She would have rather seen him marry Sharon.

"I don't care that she doesn't like me. I would have still gotten her a card. And today was a special day for Nina. I should be at her reception right now."

"So are you going to take them home or what?" he replied nonchalantly. "If you hadn't brought Larry with you, there would be more room in your car."

Ignoring his comment, I whispered in his ear, "How are you taking her out when you told me yesterday you didn't have any money?"

"Today is Sunday, Gwendolyn," Bishop replied. "I have the tithes and offerings."

With that, I just left him standing there in church. After leaving, I dropped his members off first and then my little brother, before going to my cousin's reception extremely late.

On Sunday nights, me, Ken, who was a male friend from church, and my cousin Tonya would hit a poetry club on the south side of town and a few other events. My cousin Tonya and Ken had even attended Bishop's church with me on occasion.

When I mentioned to Bishop that Tonya, Ken, and I were going to hit the poetry club, he said, "Gwendolyn, I know you like the whole spoken word scene, but if it's not a church or Christian type of event, I don't want you there. The bishop's wife can't be seen any and everywhere."

Once again, I thought to myself, *But I'm not your wife yet.*

I did stop going to certain poetry sets, but only because of the material I was hearing. Some of it was extremely raunchy, and I didn't need to fall back into any of my old ways based on what was in my ear gate. So, I would attend calmer, more wholesome poetry events.

I understood that my life would change being married to a bishop. That was another thing. He was once a bishop, but had resigned many years ago from the denomination. When I asked him if he was going to join another denomination, he said no and stated he didn't want to go back to being called pastor. My Sugar Lump was title struck like so many other people in ministry. I truly had a lot on my plate to work with.

I told my cousins Nina and Kia that I needed to take this whole new life approaching me to another level, so I asked them to take me shopping to change my look. They both have impeccable taste in clothing and agreed to help me, but Nina felt I dressed nice. My style was original, and I looked well put together, especially when I attended church.

My cousin Kia kept telling me to call her grandmother to talk to her before I married this man. When Kia showed her grandmother a picture of him, she said, "Whoa! That man looks like the devil." When Kia told me that, I was like, "Wow! What does Grandma see that I don't see?" Yet, I didn't listen to Kia and never called her grandmother.

I also reached out to a co-pastor/First Lady in another state. I had known her for a while, and every time I saw her and would hear her speak, I was just in awe. She was beautiful, talented, and very supportive of her husband. I had seen them tag team a sermon, and she was a powerhouse. I let her know what was going on with me and what was before me, then asked her if I could sit at her feet and study her. She gave me excellent advice and agreed to let me study her when the time came.

When I shared with her that my mate was caught up with the First Lady image, she explained that the American churches, especially those with an African American denomination, viewed the First Lady as some sort of superstar, and therefore, she had to portray this image by dressing and acting a certain way. The real concern after becoming a wife to a man of God should be about handling his natural and his supernatural. I even had this discussion with Bishop many times, but he still held on to that whole image of me wearing some ridiculous hat with a matching two-piece outfit and shoes. After a while, I just followed his request instead of arguing with him about it. It just seemed he was more caught up on image more so than having a wife. I have it embedded in my head that people are imperfect, but real love looks past a person's imperfections and loves them regardless, just as Christ loves us.

As always, our evenings we would hang out on Skype or Yahoo Messenger. One weekend, we were chatting on Skype, and Bishop was discussing wedding plans and coming to meet my father so he could take him out for a one-on-one to ask him for my hand in marriage. We also made arrangements to visit some jewelry stores to get sized for rings and for us to have physicals. I had just had a full physical, along with HIV/STD testing, and was given a clean bill of health besides my anemia. So, he had me to schedule him a checkup. We were truly lining up all we needed to do to become husband and wife.

The girls were home, so he had me bring them to the computer screen so they could make faces with him and act silly. He did the same in return. Then, he talked to them on a more serious note, explaining to them that he was going to marry their mother and we were going to have a nice wedding and honeymoon.

"You're going to be in the wedding and at the reception," he told them. "And both of you will have to write something nice for me to welcome me to the family. Your mom and I are going to have our own baby."

Now, the girls were excited up until the point when he

mentioned a baby.

"Another sibling!" my oldest daughter said and fell out on the floor. "I can't take another sibling."

He laughed but told them to get ready to be a family. They would now be the daughters of a bishop, so they must behave accordingly. When he informed them that we were in the process of looking for a house and once we got married they would be getting a dog, they began jumping and screaming with excitement. They were six and ten at that time, so they were still young and impressionable.

I smiled at him via the computer screen and then said, "Now about this baby ordeal. You know my tubes are tied, and honestly, I don't want any more children. We discussed a dog would be just fine."

He laughed. "Gwendolyn, you're going to be my wife. I'm the leader, and what I say goes. So, if we have to get your tubes untied, we will. Now, you need to start saving money for the wedding, honeymoon, and the platinum ring I want."

As I listened to him, I wondered where all the money for these things was going to come from.

The following Sunday, he surprised me at my church home by visiting, and my uncle let him have a few remarks at the end of the service. Everyone finally got a chance to meet the guy they heard me talk about. All the ladies asked me about him after church, and I was happy I got many compliments on his attire and the way he spoke. He said he came because he hadn't been there yet and would soon be taking me away from my church home. So, he came to meet everyone and fellowship with us.

One afternoon, Bishop was going to see one of his members that had been shot. He called and told me that upon his return, we would go out to lunch. He took forever, though, and I was trying not to be insensitive to the situation. Still, he could have called to say something or texted me. I just sat around waiting for the longest. When he finally picked me up, he had his phone in his hand and it was on speaker phone. So, I sat silently, assuming he was taking care of business.

Then I heard a woman wailing over the phone. "But I love you! I love you! I supported you! I had been there for you! What does Gwendolyn have over me! Please! Please! Please!"

I just looked at him with an incredulous expression, not believing that he picked me up and had Sharon on the phone with him. Throughout our relationship I had a problem with her. He told me that they had been friends for more than six years. Yet, I knew otherwise from the people at his church and the things he would say about her. If they were just "friends", why did she leave his church when she knew I existed? Many times, he made me feel as if I had to compete with her. She was madly in love with him and wouldn't let it go. However, at times, I felt he led her on.

Since he knew she was into him, why would he keep accepting things from her? He had told me how she had gotten a boot off of his car, paid for clothing, his church rent, car repairs, gifts…you name it. He threw her in my face often and told me that she showed how much she cared about him by her actions.

I was sick and tired of hearing about her and what she did for him and being compared to her. I went out of my way trying to please him. I didn't have the money she had, so it would never add up or top what she did for him. I gave and gave to him until I had nothing, not even a place to live because I neglected my rent to pay his and ended up losing my apartment.

When I told him what was going on with that, he told me, "Gwendolyn, you're almost my wife. You don't need an apartment of your own and all those bills. You need to save money for our wedding and honeymoon."

I tried to borrow money or do whatever I could to keep my place, but it didn't work out, and in the end, he was no help. He told me it was best for me to go stay with my mom so I could prepare to become his wife. I thought about how much I had heard about Sharon from him and others, and the mention that her house had once been in foreclosure. I believe that was because of him. She helped him so much that her mortgage got behind.

I listened to her cry about how much she loved him and bribing him by offering to replace his 1999 Benz with the current year if he left me. She was a nurse, had a house, and basically, he could have a good life with her. She continued crying and pleading with him during our entire ride to the restaurant, while he just listened to her go on and on. I was angry as hell, yet I never said a word. As we entered the restaurant, he finally ended the call. After we were seated, I guess he noticed the look on my face that could have literally killed him.

"Gwendolyn, she's in love with me, and she's been there for me. So, when she calls, I can't be mean to her. I have to help her heal from this."

Is he serious? I thought to myself.

I looked at him and said, "So whoever is in love with you, they can call and cry in your ear until they feel better?"

His response was, "Well, all the women in my past have a hard time getting over me. My ex-wives cried for years about me. Sharon has a hard time accepting this, so I'm trying to be there for her."

By this time, I think steam was coming from my ears. He

came around the table, sat next to me, and tried to kiss me. I refused him, leaning away from him, and he went back to his side of the table.

"I have something to tell you about Sharon," he said.

"YOU SLEPT WITH HER!" was my initial response.

"Gwendolyn, lower your voice. My wife doesn't yell in public places, and no, I did not sleep with her. When I was on my way to see the young man who had been shot, she came by my apartment to drop off some books that she had of mine. So, I had her take me to the hospital."

I jumped up and tried to walk out the restaurant, but he grabbed my arm and whispered in my ear, "You're making a scene. My wife does not act like this. Sit down and listen to me."

So, I sat down, looking at him with tears in my eyes.

He continued. "The whole ride she was begging me to kiss her, but I kept refusing. She was saying, 'You kiss Gwendolyn. Now kiss me.' When she brought me back home, she wouldn't let me out of her car. She grabbed me and forced me to kiss her."

When he stopped talking, the tears I was trying so desperately to hold back were now streaming down my face.

"How does a grown man let anyone force a kiss on him?" I asked calmly. "Men are naturally stronger than woman, so how could you not stop her? Plus, you know how she feels about you.

So why even put yourself in a situation to be alone with her? You seem as if you like drama and leading her on."

"I know, Gwendolyn. I'm sorry," he repeated over and over.

I didn't even eat my food. I had nothing more to say, not even in the car heading back home.

Once we were in the car, he asked did I mind if he stopped at the store to pick up a few things. I told him no, but I didn't go inside the store with him. I stayed in the car, where he also left his phone. Unable to resist being nosy after all that had transpired, I started going through his call log. Just like Mama said, 'If you go looking for something, you'll find it.' There were many calls placed between him and Sharon. My blood was boiling now. Then I looked at his text messages, and there was Sharon's name again. What was even more disturbing was the text exchange between him and a guy who was also a preacher.

Preacher: What are your plans for the evening?

Bishop: Nothing much. What's up?

Preacher: Want some cum?

Bishop: ☺…Sure

Preacher: Okay…will pick you up about nine.

Bishop: Should be a quiet night. The women are mad at me.

Now I had found more than I wanted to find. I was so used to this behavior in the church that it shouldn't have shocked me.

I just thought he was one who wouldn't be a part of that foolishness.

What the hell have I gotten myself into? I thought as he approached the car. I tried to erase any expression from my face and didn't say a word. I couldn't let him know I went snooping through his phone. When we reached my house, I asked him when he would be going to get his physical because I wanted the whole report before walking down the aisle.

He smiled and simply said, "Okay, Gwendolyn. I'll call you later."

As I walked in the house, I broke down into tears and started thinking about the few episodes we had, thankful that I had never slept with him. Then I got down on my knees and began praying hard about that man. *God, please tell me this ain't so. I love him. I need him. Please don't let this be happening. I've given up too much to let this go down the drain. Lord, show him to me.*

I cried until I fell asleep. When he called later that night, I asked him was that homosexual and promiscuous demon completely out of him. He said yes and then asked why I was asking again. I responded by telling him that I just wanted to be sure and hear him say it again.

One Monday evening, Sugar Lump called and told me that he was having a church meeting he wanted me to attend and for me to dress nice. So, I picked out a pair of summer green pants, a green and white blouse, and matching accessories. I dropped the girls off at my mother's house and headed to the meeting.

The meeting dealt with church issues. I'm sure all pastors have to put fires out every once in a while. I sat in the meeting taking notes as if it were my church home. At the end of the meeting, Bishop called me up in front of his congregation and began on the subject of gossip.

"People call my mother and tell her things. You all have private discussions about what you think is going on in my life, but y'all don't know. Haven't you all heard me say for years that I'm not getting married? I have said it time and time again."

His flock was in agreement with having heard him say that numerous times.

"Well, that was until I met Gwendolyn."

They all began to awww and clap.

He continued. "Gwendolyn Jackson has agreed to date this old man. We are boyfriend and girlfriend. We're in the process of getting to know all we can about each other so we can move to the next status of becoming engaged, and when I propose, it won't be a secret. I will do it right here in front of all of you."

He then went on to brag about how I was sick and he brought me some medicine, drove me to work when my car broke down, came to my church home, met my parents…on and on.

"I already love Gwendolyn. She is helpful and supportive of me. I want you all to give her the same respect and honor you give me. I shouldn't hear any more gossip after tonight. You all know now that this is my girlfriend. This could very well be y'alls First Lady soon."

Everyone began clapping, and once the meeting was over, they all hugged me and offered their congratulations. Bishop hugged me tight as we left church and went our separate ways home.

It was one month later, and I had remained faithful, supportive, loyal, understanding, and did all I could for him in spite of things that were in the back of my head. On a Tuesday night in his bible class, he bragged about how I never quit on him, how I stayed up late working with him in ministry, and how I was always there for him, never telling him no. Two days later on a Thursday, he broke up with me over Skype.

Chapter 2:
Stages of Release
Loose it & let it go…Not that simple.

I'll never forget that Thursday evening when Bishop and I were communicating via instant messenger, as usual. In the middle of our chat, he began telling me that he wanted to end our relationship. Stage one: shock. This is a natural reaction when one isn't expecting something to happen. I looked at my computer with a strange look, thinking he was joking, while he continued to say he didn't have time to wait for me to get to where he wanted me to be in life. He wanted someone who was already there.

When I asked him where was I exactly, he sent back the following message: *You don't have a degree; you got laid off; you don't own any property; and you're not in ministry. You don't have all it takes to be married to a bishop.*

Stage two: disbelief. I couldn't believe him. I called him repeatedly, but he wouldn't answer. So, I went back to the computer and sent him a few messages. Still, he wouldn't respond.

Next, I got in my car and just started crying. For the first time in my life, I cried over a relationship. I've been hurt before, but I always managed to hold it together. I called my evangelist friend, whom was his member. I was crying so hard that she couldn't understand what I was saying. So, she just started praying for me and trying to calm me down. Finally, I was able to tell her what had taken place. Afterwards, I drove around for a bit while still crying.

I finally pulled over and called my cousin Cee-Cee. She tried to calm me, but of course, she was angry, too, because her cousin was hurting over a man that she knew wasn't good for me.

Stage three: sorrow. I couldn't shake off the pain. I drove to a nearby park, where I cried harder while so many thoughts raced through my head.

Then came the period of blaming self, which is stage four. *What did I do wrong? Should I have done more? Maybe he did want sex and wanted me to initiate it. Maybe my children were too much for him.*

My best friend Sharron was walking past the park to pick her children up from school, when she saw me crying and came over to comfort me. I got out of my car and walked to her kids' school with her. While on the way, I told her what I was dealing with and how I was puzzled by his sudden decision because I didn't understand what I had done to him. Now, Sharron is the type who gets upset if someone she loves gets hurt by another. She was pissed off, wanting to cut his head off, and at the time, I would have helped her.

When I returned home, I lay down and cried for the remainder of the night. I begged God to change his heart and mend our relationship. I prayed and cried until the morning hours.

The next day, I drove to the park that I used to take my children to in the neighborhood where we once lived, which was also near Bishop's house. I texted him and asked him to come meet me so we could talk face to face since he dumped me over Skype. He took his time about coming, but he finally showed up. When he arrived, he asked if it was safe to get in my car. I guess he thought I was going to attack him or something since he was dealing with a woman scorned. I just wanted more of an explanation and some closure, which is stage five.

"So you just woke up yesterday and decided you no longer wanted to be with me?" I asked. "On Tuesday, you were bragging to your members in bible class about how I stay up late laboring for your ministry," I added. My emotions still had the best of me, but I refused to let him see me cry.

"Gwendolyn, you're a great girlfriend. You've dated many men, and all you were good enough to be was a girlfriend. None of them married you, so why did you think I'd be any different?"

My mouth was wide open. I couldn't believe what he had said to me and the lack of truth behind it. I had been proposed to twice and couldn't believe he was throwing that in my face. I couldn't help but cry then. Laying my head on my steering wheel, I started to weep while he just sat there looking.

Then he said, "Gwendolyn, you were supposed to do the things you did for me. Truth is, I can have anyone do those things for me. In fact, I have had women who have done more by buying me mink coats and designer suits. When you're in a relationship, you do those things for your mate."

"Well, hell, I only received two cards and some cough medicine from you," I replied. "I earned my spot in your life, while you deceived your way into mine. Everything I've done and sacrificed meant nothing to you. Working alongside you in ministry wasn't the easiest job, but I held it down, and at times, better than you. What about the times when I would buy your groceries every month, pay your rent, create your flyers, do miscellaneous things for the church, and all the time I invested in you?"

All he could say is I was supposed to do all that. I was sitting there thinking, *This fool told me relationships are supposed to be mutually beneficial.* So, I approached the relationship wondering what I could give to help this person and prove my love to him, while he just looked at me as another woman to take advantage of.

He then told me again why he no longer wanted me for a wife. To which I replied, "You were my friend for more than a year before we dated, so you knew what I had and who I was. Yet, you still chose me. That alone lets me know you were phony from the start. You asked me to be in your life as more than a friend. I didn't ask you."

Then after all this bull, he had the audacity to ask me if we could remain friends. I told him no. I was too hurt to be his friend. If I remained his friend, I'd never get him out of my system. It's easy to turn a friendship into a relationship, but a relationship into a friendship? No way can I do that.

After he got out of my car to get into his, I exited mine and walked over to sit on a park bench. As he drove by, he said, "I don't have many friends, Gwendolyn. Don't do this to me. We can at least be friends."

I just looked in disgust, and then after he was out of sight, I sat there and cried my eyes out. I finally went home, and over the next few weeks, I sunk into a deep depression - stage six.

I cried every day, all day and all night. It was hard trying to hide the pain from my daughters, and they would catch me crying from time to time. I even made a video for him using my webcam, begging him to not let us end like this. I cried out to him while trying to get my words out. It was a constant plea, but to no avail. He still was heartless and let me know again that I didn't have what it takes to be a bishop's wife. My oldest daughter, the fireball, began saying things about wanting to hurt him since he hurt her mother. I had even stopped eating. I asked God over and over why. My relationship wasn't sinful. I didn't sleep with him before marriage, lie to him, or anything. We studied the word together, prayed together, and laughed together. I supported him in everything, and he left me for what I lacked.

Crying, I grabbed a bottle of prescription-strength Tylenol and walked to the bathroom. No one was home, and with at least ten pills in my hand and a face covered in tears, I looked in the mirror and said goodbye to myself, preparing to take my life. Just as I found the courage to take the pills, the dog jumped all over me, and being weak from not eating and sleeping, I fell into the tub and the pills fell out of my hand. I guess it's true that pets can sense when something is wrong.

As I sat on the side of the tub, I picked the pills up and flushed them down the toilet. Then, I got on my knees and apologized to God because I knew better. I got back in the bed, while still crying.

As the days went on, I cried less. Yet, my heart still ached. I reached out to him again via Skype and Yahoo messenger, but he totally ignored me.

By now, I was at stage seven: acceptance. I attempted to accept it, recollect myself, and get my life back on track. The day finally came when I stopped crying and never shed another tear. Keep in mind, though, this was a period of time over a few months.

Something on the shelf inside of me fell off and shattered. It was him. I literally felt a breaking inside of me. I was broken and had to be put back together again.

Chapter 3:
Red Flags
Honey, how did you miss that?

We often hear the term red flag as part of the National Weather Service's warning. We also hear the term in the dating world. In some cases, I believe the term "red banner" should be used. Banners are bigger than flags. They're huge. So, honey, how could you miss that?

Ladies, do not ignore certain signs a man gives you. I don't care how smooth he talks, how good he looks, or how intellectual he may seem. Remove the scales and open your eyes. If I had done this from the jump, I never would have let the relationship go as far as it did. I should have put my running shoes on, pretended I was Jackie Joyner-Kersee, and ran like Forrest Gump clear across country. Remove the scales and open your eyes so you can focus. Sometimes there is a red banner attached to a helicopter that is circling your place of residence and telling you to run, yet we still ignore it. I sure did!

One evening, Bishop and I were up late chatting via phone, and he brought up the fact that I once dated a much older man and the fact that my children's fathers are much older than I am. Certainly, this was nothing new to him. He knew this while he was just my friend, so why he decided to bring it up again I have no clue.

"Well, I'm sure everything that has happened in your life you don't brag about," I replied. "So, tell me what's something you did, but don't really know why you did it."

He began telling me that he had been to jail a few times for having sex with underage girls. He told me this story with very little remorse, which led to me asking my next question.

"What drove you to do that?"

He said the girls were after him, and when the judge questioned him, all the evidence proved the teen girls pursued him. I was in awe listening to him.

Now, I'm not saying Gwendolyn has been a perfect little angel, because I have some stories of my own. Nor am I saying people can't change, because surely they can. I just couldn't believe he thought his actions were justifiable because the girls were after him. *Come on, Bishop, you knew better.* Plus, he was in ministry already when these things occurred.

When I asked why he divorced, he said his ex-wife lost trust in him because he spent too much time doing ministry. However, after we dated for a while, it came out that he had done some things his wife was not approving of, such as seeing another girl in the ministry and buying gifts for one woman who was also married. He even got his tires slashed by another woman.

Still, what did Gwendolyn do? I chose to see the good in him. Yet, Sharon was on the scene even when I came on, and he used her for six years, accepting gifts, money, and whatever else he could get from her. She was crazy about him! Sometimes when I would be with him, she would call him crying, and he would put the call on speakerphone so I could listen to this other woman cry over him. Then, he would laugh about it! Y'all are probably thinking, *Gwendolyn, you had plenty of time to run like hell.* Yet, I stayed!

The red banners were there and had always been there. They may not be noticeable in the beginning, but keep your eyes and ears open. Of course, when the first date and first few phone calls occur, you still may not notice them. Most people won't say or do anything to make themselves look bad in the beginning, but as time goes on, don't ignore the obvious. I made some huge mistakes in this area. When he spoke, I listened to him with that smooth talk, and then he'd flip to Mr. Intellectual and throw in scripture here and there. I was blind and deaf. This is a big no-no!

If you're more thoughtful than your mate, this is a sign. For example, whenever I would go to the grocery store or office supply store, I would ask Bishop if he needed anything, and normally he would give me a list. Yet, he lived five minutes away from me, and whenever he went out his door, he never bothered to ask if there was something he could pick up for me while he was out. This is a sign, ladies. This is a thoughtless person. Only when it comes down to him does anything matter…no matter how great or small.

Numerous times, I would pull up to his apartment building with dinner, groceries, work he had given me to do, or items he had asked me to pick up while at the store, and guess what? I was never ALLOWED in his apartment, not the whole time I dated him. Whenever I asked why I couldn't come in, he would tell me it wasn't time for me to come into his home yet. Now this man had been in every room in my apartment and spent countless hours there, so how in the world was it that I wasn't allowed in his? Being naïve, I thought, *Well, he is a bishop. Maybe it doesn't seem right for his lady to be in his apartment.* Yet, when you're floating on cloud nine, you don't see the "obvious" things. To anyone who is reading this, I'm begging you to open your eyes, especially when it seems too good to be true.

Pay attention to the relationships he has with other people. Watch how he treats those who he is not trying to impress. Take notice of how he treats the people he says he loves like family.

When I met Bishop, he told me that he had three biological sons. Once we got close, I found out he had absolutely nothing to do with his own children. He explained to me the disagreements, issues, and whatever. Still, I couldn't understand how he could claim to be this mighty man of God and want to parent other people's children, but have nothing to do with his own. He even had the nerve to challenge me on my parenting skills.

Once, his youngest son called to wish him a Happy Father's Day, and all Bishop said was, "Thank you," and then hung up with no further conversation. Now here was a teen reaching out to his father, who is a man of God and loves to throw scripture in the air about "with love and kindness have I drawn thee," yet he hung up as if he could care less that the call was even made. It was his chance to truly operate as a father, and he allowed the opportunity to slip by.

He also has two adult sons that he hasn't spoken to or seen in years. There has been drama between them, but what family doesn't have their share of drama? I'm friends with his oldest son on Facebook and we chat often, whereas his own father doesn't extend the olive branch. That's clearly something I shouldn't have ignored.

Another red banner I ignored was when he discussed marrying me and I asked who was going to do our premarital counseling. He had the audacity to tell me, "I'm the bishop. I don't need counseling. Do you think Bishop Jakes, Bishop Morton, or Bishop Noel Jones would go through counseling?"

I responded by telling him, "I would imagine so. A counselor can explore deep areas that we may overlook."

Yet, he insisted he didn't need counseling. He felt I was the one that needed counseling and that he was doing fine at bringing me up to his level! This was something else I ignored at the time and wish I hadn't. Warning comes before destruction, and it came to me numerous times. Still, I didn't pay attention. Some things were major and should not have been overlooked.

When dating, ladies, please open your eyes and ears.

Watch how the man treats people he's not trying to impress.

Watch how he treats his parents, children, and even animals.

Pay attention to the company he keeps or does not keep.

Is he caring or controlling?

Is he chivalrous or does he leave you hanging?

Does he compliment you or does he look to always be complimented?

Is he giving or are you the one that does all the giving?

Does he listen when something is bothering you and offers great advice, or does he tell you to get over it and focus your attention back on him?

Is this relationship mutually beneficial or one-sided?

I can't stress this enough: Ladies AND men, please pay attention to EVERYTHING. Of course, most relationships start out beautiful and everyone is on their best behavior. However, when the guards slowly come down, get out of the fuzzy feeling of being on cloud nine. Close the book of emotions and use your senses, especially your vision and hearing. Some of these things you don't have to get all deep and spiritual about. Just pay close attention. Stop wearing your emotions on your sleeve, especially when they don't match your outfit anyway. Use that sixth sense of common sense.

I wanted to be loved so badly, finally settle down, and get married that I dummied down my intellect and turned off my mental radar, allowing complete foolery into my life. Don't ever settle for less!

Chapter 4:
I Fell In Love with a Stripper
Nope, not the song.

    I watched my father pull up an old carpet when my mother decided to redecorate. As he pulled up the old, dusty, brown rug, it revealed a warped, uneven shabby wooden floor underneath. Yet, Daddy was not done stripping the floor. He got a scraper and began to scrape all the uneven spaces of the floor to make sure there was absolutely nothing left on it, just completely bare.

    I said all that to say I fell in love with a stripper. No, Bishop didn't dance on a pole with a G-string. Yet, he stripped me until I was down to nothing, just like the floor. Being in love sometimes can be blinding. Whatever Bishop said or wanted, Gwendolyn went right along with it.

    Now, I was the type of woman who served in a ministry to whatever capacity needed. I was the director over three different ministries and assisted others. My work in ministry was never for me to be seen or have my name called like so many people operate. Instead, it was a passion for me. It made me feel good to work in the church; it was joyous.

One day, Bishop told me that charity starts at home.

"What are you trying to say, Sugar Lump?" I asked him.

He replied, "When we're studying the word of God, I feel you're not where you need to be spiritually because of what I have to teach you. You should have known these things."

"Well, your teachings and my pastor's teachings are different," I responded. "That's the same as if I read a scripture. The revelation I get may not be the same one you get."

Then he continued by saying, "While I'm talking to you or over your house, you're adding your pastor's clips on YouTube and booking guests for a show. You're just too busy in the church, and if you're going to marry a bishop, you have to learn charity starts at home. So, I come first. I need you to sit down, absorb the word, and let others work. If you're going to work in ministry, it should be for me."

So guess what Gwendolyn did? I sat down on something I was so passionate about. He stripped a part of who I was, and I allowed him to be based on the person I thought he was and that he would make me his wife one day.

One night as I was getting ready to attend a musical, Bishop said to me, "You can't go. My wife will not be seen any- and everywhere nor come in all hours of the night."

It was a church musical that started at seven o'clock! Seriously, how late could it go? Even though I wasn't his wife yet, again I allowed him to keep me from doing something I wanted to do.

In the middle of the year, I got laid off my job due to the recession. I didn't panic, though. Those things happen. In fact, I was okay with it because it freed up my days for me to work on some other things while I collected unemployment. Sometimes after dropping my children off at school, just being nice, I would ride by Bishop's house to take him some coffee. Then I would go home and maybe enjoy a nap or watch some television. It was those times Bishop would call and tell me that I was not being productive.

"Do you think Michelle Obama takes naps?" he would say. "No, she's helping her man be successful."

While that may or may not have been true, he wasn't Obama. He didn't work himself. He was at home watching television or whatever he wanted to do with his time, yet he would ride me. So, as my time off work went on, he would tell me things that he needed done and wanted me to do. My free time soon turned into "his" time. He would ask me to create flyers, pluggers, make phone calls, design t-shirts, and once, he even called to have me surf the net and do research for his bible class. Next thing I knew instead of having a man, I felt like I had a boss. I spent my days working for him.

Every time I would get my unemployment check, I would run to Wal-Mart, like most women, and purchase things for the household, as well as run errands, pay bills, and possibly treat the kids to a little something. Bishop called one particular day, and when he asked what I was doing, I told him that I was getting ready to take the kids to Chuck E. Cheese.

"Oh yeah? What's the occasion?" he asked.

"Nothing," I replied, "just taking them out because I want to do something nice for them."

"Gwendolyn, you're doing unnecessary stuff with your money," Bishop started to preach, and not in a good way. "You have a man in your life now, and when you're dating a bishop, you must know that you have to take care of him. How many pastors do you know with a job beyond the church, yet their wives have jobs and carry the weight of whatever the church doesn't? I only have about fifteen members, so you have to help me. I told you how the women in my past helped me."

Next thing I knew, all my stuff was behind. However, his rent was paid, his old Benz was running well, he wore the finest clothes, his cell phone was active, his cable was on, and he had a full tank of gas in his car. All while Gwendolyn sank. I fell behind in my rent, lights, gas, phone, cable…everything.

As I stated earlier, when I told him about my struggles, he suggested I give up my apartment and move in with my mother.

"How do I know you're serious about me without signs of preparation? So, moving in with your mother would be best," he had said.

It's not like I had much of a choice anyway since I had gotten too far behind on my rent to catch up. It just seemed like he didn't care what was happening to me. After you've been on your own, it's extremely hard to move back home to your parents' house. Faced with no other alternative, though, I ended up doing just that. Still, when check day rolled around, he would come by to pick up money for his rent, or I would call in his phone payment, or go to the store and get whatever he needed.

I fell in love with a stripper that stripped everything from me…my passions, my hobbies, me working in ministry, my finances, and even my time. I had nothing left at all for Gwendolyn once we were over. He stripped it all and I allowed it. "Anything allowed is permission to continue," was one of his favorite sayings. I allowed this foolishness for so long that it left me with nothing. I gave up so much of myself for him.

I'm not saying two people in a relationship are not supposed to compromise, but there is a huge difference between making compromises for your mate and losing yourself.

Chapter 5:
Change vs. Compromise
Ever given up sense of who you are to be with someone else?

Ever felt as if you've sacrificed or changed to accommodate your mate so much that you've lost sense of who you are? His/her likes start to be your likes, and your world revolves around making him/her happy. You lost the total essence of who you are and what you like. Now you've been molded into what your mate likes and expects from you.

In relationships, there will always be some compromising and even a little bit of change. This is totally fine. However, when you change from being seventy-five percent of the person you were for your mate, it makes you wonder why they were attracted to you in the first place if they molded you into someone else. OOOH WEEE! I mean, we've all heard of the 80/20 rule, but did the brother really only like twenty percent of you and had to create his other eighty percent? Have you ever found yourself doing, saying, and participating in things that totally were not you nor did you agree with them? I sure did!

I have a vibrant, bubbly personality, and ninety percent of the time I always have a smile on my face. I love to make people laugh, and I love to engage in intellectual conversations. I thank God for my personality. I'm one who doesn't have any problems making friends, and my friends can always feel comfortable with being themselves around me. I am still a saved woman of God, just one with a vibrant personality who doesn't judge.

In this relationship with Bishop, change versus compromise never applied to us. Point blank, Gwendolyn had to change to be with him. The issues I would point out to him about *him*, he never budged on any of them. So here it is, a woman who loved him and was being honest with him about his arrogant attitude, his approach toward his flock, and his lack of not doing what he should have been doing, and he didn't want to take heed. Instead, he would stress his age to me, which was forty-three years old, and tell me that what I said was irrelevant because he had lived life, been there and done that.

"No matter how old you are or what you've been through, you never stop learning," I responded. "Then when it comes to me, you feel so much needs to be changed about me in order to be with you. You're not asking me to compromise or meet you halfway. You're asking me to totally change who I am. And not only that, you're asking for me to change overnight."

He said I was too common with his members, but my personality is just like that with whomever. I'm an extrovert, and he was an introvert. You would think that would be a balanced relationship, right? Of course, he didn't see it that way. He wanted me to back up some from being friendly with his members, which I didn't do because I had become close with a few of them. He never had the willingness to compromise or change on anything. Yet, I still loved him. Neither of us was perfect, but real love sees an imperfect person perfectly. Therefore, in my eyes, he wasn't always right, but he was just right for me. The sad thing was he didn't believe that the way I did.

I was so in love with him that I would call out his flaws and tell him he needed to adjust some things. I gave him loving CORRECTION for his DIRECTION because he was hindering his PROGRESSION. It's one thing to try and change a person to what you want them to be, and it's totally different if you see someone failing in areas and you do nothing to advise them of a better way. A lot of people say don't try and change people. I can only agree with that statement to a certain extent. Some of the things he told me about myself really helped me once I adjusted them. When you're in school, you can be a great student, but the teacher corrects you on things so you can be better in the long run.

I already stated how my personality is. I am a mother, daughter, sister, aunt, niece, friend, poet, and servant. In this relationship with Bishop, I was not allowed to wear all the hats that I possess.

My class reunion was being held one weekend, with a party, picnic, and more planned. Wanting to attend the festivities, I purchased tickets for me and my older brother. Needless to say, when Bishop found out, he was dead set about me not going to the party.

"Oh no!" he said. "No woman of mine will be at a party. You don't know who may see you. They're going to say the bishop's woman was at a party."

Clearly, I didn't go to parties on a regular basis. However, this was my class reunion, and I wanted to see my classmates. Surely, I know how to conduct myself as a lady at all times. So, I didn't think it mattered about me being at the party as long my conduct and behavior was ladylike while at the event. I don't drink, so I didn't see why it was such a big deal.

When I invited him to come with me, he said, "I'm the bishop. I can't be seen at a party. Are you serious?" Then he added, "When we get married, are you going to disobey my orders or listen to me?"

So, the money I spent on the ticket went down the drain and I stayed at home. The next day, he did allow me to go to the picnic, but I had to be home by a certain time. Who does that? Yet, he would say that he wasn't changing me, only protecting me. If he was so worried about protecting me, why not attend events with me?

I dress nice and ladylike, but he seemed to always find a problem with my appearance. To him, my skirts need to be longer, long-sleeve shirts were a must, my hair couldn't be too long, and wearing flip-flops were out of the question. In addition, I had to be aware of the volume of my laugh. "Don't laugh too loudly in public," he would say.

All of these were changes he put on me and more. He molded me into what he wanted me to be, which made me wonder what he liked about me in the beginning, if anything at all.

One day, I looked at myself in the mirror and didn't even recognize myself. I was no longer the Gwendolyn everyone knew. I wasn't even the Gwendolyn that I knew. I would be at home watching television by myself and find myself cracking up with laughter. Then I would stop and quiet down because I would remember what he said about laughing too loudly. Even when I wasn't with him, I would find myself under the control of him.

It's definitely okay to compromise in relationships. I know one day I will marry and have to compromise. However, to change who I am totally for my mate is just something I shouldn't have done. I am sure there is someone who will love my personality, appreciate that I have my own hobbies, and even love my laugh. So, to you reading this, please don't lose yourself in another person, because once they're gone, what do you have left?

Chapter 6:
Forgiveness

*Forgiveness is setting someone free
& finding out that person was you!*

As I was working on this book, it took me longer to complete it than I thought. I have a friend who is also an author, and while we were having lunch one day, I asked for his writing advice. I told him that I was struggling with writing the first chapter of this book. I had to tell how my relationship started out beautiful, or at least that's how I viewed it in the beginning.

My friend, Ben, simply said, "Gwendolyn, you haven't forgiven him. You say you have, but you truly haven't. If you had forgiven him already, you would be able to write with the spirit of forgiveness."

I couldn't do anything but respect what he was telling me because he was right. When you have fully forgiven a person, you can be in their presence and not get upset. You can even converse as civil adults with one another. Even more so, you can pray for the person who has wronged you.

Now I'm certain many people have heard this over and over. Forgiveness is more for you than the other person. That statement is very true, and so is the statement, 'Holding on to unforgiveness is like holding hot coals in your hand. You're the only one who gets burned.'

I would talk to my friends Ariel and Cassandra, who I love dearly, and of course by them being members of his church, they would talk about him often. My ears would burn at just the mention of his name. I even started avoiding some of their calls just so I wouldn't hear his name. When I would flip through the television channels and run across him preaching on the religious channel, I would want to throw up and hoped he would choke on his words because he didn't live up to them. All of these antics of mine were childish and nothing more than me still holding that pain in my heart.

I know everyone has been hurt by the actions or words of another. Even I have hurt other people. Hurt is universal. These wounds can leave you with long-lasting feelings of anger, bitterness, and even vengeance if you don't practice forgiveness. You may be the one in the long run who pays for it. By embracing forgiveness, you embrace peace, hope, gratitude, and you restore joy back into your life.

It's certainly not easy to just forgive and forget. Generally, forgiveness is a decision to let go of resentment and thoughts of revenge. After everything Bishop had done to me, I had thoughts of revenge. There was so much I could have done to him, and I had access to do it. Yet, I didn't act on it even though the thoughts crossed my mind. The act that hurt or offended you will always remain a part of your life, but forgiveness can lessen its grip on you and help you focus on other positive parts of your life. Forgiveness can even lead to the feelings of understanding, empathy, and compassion for the one who hurt you.

Forgiveness doesn't mean you forget or that you deny the other person's responsibility for hurting you. It doesn't minimize or justify the wrong. You can forgive the person without excusing the act of what they have done. Forgiveness brings a kind of peace over you that will help you to go on with your life.

When you're hurt by someone you love and trust, you become angry, sad, or even confused. I experienced all of these things. If you dwell on hurtful events or situations, grudges filled with resentment, vengeance, and hostility may take root. If you allow negative feelings to push out your positive feelings, you may find yourself swallowed up by your own bitterness or sense of injustice.

I got so caught up in bitterness that I cut out just about everyone in my life for a period of time because I let the resentment against him trickle over into every other relationship I had with people. I barely spoke with many of my family members and friends.

Forgive the other party. As I stated, at the very sound of his name I wanted to throw up, or throw darts at his face whenever I would see him. I even felt like that song and wanted to bust the windows out of his Benz. I was mad as hell at him. Thankfully, I didn't act on my thoughts, but I had to do what my friend, Ben, told me to do, which was to truthfully and wholeheartedly forgive him. So, I got down on my knees in my room and told God exactly how I was feeling. No deep prayer, just God and I; and I prayed these words:

Dear God, my heart has been hurt very badly. I never thought I would feel this pain again after losing many dear loved ones like my mother, my brother, and others, Lord. I had that feeling again and it hurts, Lord. It hurts. It's time I release this into your hands. Help me forgive him, Lord, and move on. I need this for me, Lord. I'm confessing it with my mouth. This time it is for real. I forgive him and I have turned my pain over to you. In your son's Jesus' name, I pray. Amen.

And with that prayer, I released that thing seriously and began to feel better. I even started to gain back some of the weight I had lost from being depressed. I went from being 160 pounds down to 141 pounds, but slowly, the weight is coming back.

Three days later, he sent a message to my Facebook account wishing me and my children a Happy New Year, and at that moment, I knew I had truly forgiven him. I smiled when I saw the message and responded cheerfully with well wishes for the New Year for him, as well. I told him to latch on to God like never before.

Forgiving him truly set me free. Free in my mind, my spirit, my body, and my soul. There is nothing like being free and released from things that once had you bound. I'm happier, healthier, and feeling great since truly forgiving him. The benefits of forgiving someone can lead to future healthier relationships, greater spiritual and psychological well-being, and less stress and hostility. I know unforgiveness can make you sick. I stayed sick for a while. Forgiveness is about setting someone free, and that person is you. Free yourself!

Forgive yourself! There may have been a time where you possibly experienced a season of self-blame. I blamed myself constantly for the loss of this relationship and often wondered what I could have done differently. I went on and on blaming myself. This is tormenting to one's self.

Forgiving yourself is essential. We all have a tendency to hold ourselves more accountable than we do others. Perhaps you're like me, wanting to justify forgiving others for whatever it is that they may have done to you. Yet, you find no justification for forgiving yourself. Life is full of choices, and every choice we make will either take us in a positive, life-giving direction or rob us of the opportunity to be a life-giving individual. If you can find it in your heart to forgive others, then surely you can find the compassion in your heart to forgive yourself. Forgiving yourself will change the direction of your life. Forgive yourself and let the healing begin.

Chapter 7:
Moving Right Along
Don't be afraid when the next man wants to date you.

After going through this ordeal with Bishop, I didn't want to be bothered with a man period, especially men in any capacity of ministry. Before he and I began dating, the only men that approached me were deacons, ministers, overseers, and such. I tried for the longest to avoid them, but it was hard considering the circles I was in. If a man was going to choose me, he would more than likely meet me at some kind of church event.

As my relationship ended with Bishop, the men of God came at me like I was passing out something for free—bishops, overseers, pastors, elders, etc., some of whom I didn't even know were in ministry. Of course, I ran. I deleted some of them as Facebook friends, and if people saw me at various church functions, I would ease out before they ended so I could avoid anyone catching me to talk to me. I definitely didn't want to be bothered with anybody in ministry. I didn't care if they were a bench member. I ran. I was still scarred from him. I felt like if you could be a bishop and not do right by a woman, then surely the rest of them were going to do me even worse. In fact, when I expressed to a few people that only men of clergy talked to me, some said you attract what you are. Someone even said that the aroma of my ex was still on me.

I don't believe his aroma is still on me. Yet, I do believe the counterfeit comes before the real thing. So, he came, and now a real man of God will come along. I no longer run from men of clergy. I just face the fact that's what I attract. I'm mostly seen in a ministry setting, so if they're watching me, then that's where they'll find me. God isn't going to place just anybody in my life because of who I am now.

Of course you have to give yourself time to regroup and heal before jumping from one relationship to the next. For almost a year, I was single by choice. I had to truly take time to get him out of my system before I could move on. When the time came for me to date and love again, I didn't hold back based on what Bishop did to me. In fact, I love harder. With the lifestyle I lead, there is a strong possibility it will be a man of God and someone involved in some form of ministry. Besides, I wouldn't want someone who is not saved and active in their church home. That's exactly what happened to me. A great man that is amazingly wonderful entered my life, and I don't have to be anyone but Gwendolyn with him. He allows me to be who I am and loves me for me. Maybe there will be a sequel written titled *When a Man of God Loves You.*

So when the man of God, man in ministry, or man period approaches you, don't be afraid once you're ready to date again. Now, dating after a failed relationship is never easy. There are so many emotions you are dealing with. Disappointment, rejection, anger, and depression can affect how you feel about finding someone new. If you have recently broken off a relationship with someone that was long term, it is especially difficult to get back into the dating game.

Allow time to reflect on your past relationship. One of the worst things to do is move on when you haven't healed from the last relationship. The aroma of the last person is still present and all over you. So, don't spread it on to the next. Their scent, your scent, and your ex's scent surely will stink! Before considering a new relationship, give yourself time to heal and get over the negative feelings. Please don't take the past hurt into the new. Don't hold the new mate accountable for what the last mate did.

If you don't allow yourself time to adjust, you will not be ready to move on. If you move too quickly, you risk hurting another person, and let's face it: hurt people…hurt people.

There's nothing worse than finding a new person but bringing baggage into that new relationship. You also don't want the new person in your life to feel as if they don't measure up to the person you dated before them. Bishop did this to me, and he also did it to the woman he dated after me. He always compared me to the person before me — what she did, how she did it — and I found myself trying to outdo whatever she had done to please him. Competing with someone who he was not with anymore was completely foolish. Don't make the mistake of always comparing the ex to the next. Dating on the rebound is not productive.

Keep in mind that once you start dating again, you don't need to rush into a serious relationship. Also, don't stereotype the people you meet before getting to know them. I've had to tell myself this very thing time after time. All men of God are not like Bishop. That was just one bad apple. Just because I meet people in the same profession doesn't mean they are the same. Certainly all men are different, so don't judge them by their titles or professions.

Enjoy your newfound freedom. It's healthy to take a timeout. Many people have made the mistake of jumping right back into a relationship. Some people are afraid of being alone. In my case, I was a person that struggled with loneliness and low self-esteem. So, I would go from one dude to the next, not allowing myself healing and closure. This kind of fear can at times cause you to meet the wrong person because of vulnerability. All of us have an innate desire to be with someone, but we have to be careful in choosing who the next person will be. Don't be desperate and thirsty because someone is smiling at you or poking you on Facebook.

Once you're ready to move on and start dating, go slow. As my uncle would say, 'Slowly peel back the layers of the onion'. Learn as much as you can about the other person. Uncover them layer by layer. Keep a positive attitude and God first. Eventually, you will have someone special.

Think a guy has the potential to be Mr. Right? Before you leap without looking, take an honest inventory. See how many of the following five essential traits he possesses.

- *Dating Trait #1: He listens to you*

What's the best way to know if Mr. Next is interested in (and worthy of) being a candidate for Mr. Right? He listens to you. You'll know he's listening when he shows genuine concern, consistently remembers things you've told him (your birthday, favorite food, best friend's name, etc.), and offers emotional support in honest and thoughtful ways.

- *Dating Trait #2: He connects with you easily*

We've all been in those relationships that take W-O-R-K (and suck the life force out of us in the process). When a relationship works on its own, it feels effortless, easy, and fluid. You don't have to force anything, forgive anyone, or turn a blind eye to red flags or gut-twisters. Instead, you communicate and collaborate with comfort, compatibility, and undeniable chemistry. If and when you experience this kind of interaction, you are on to something really special.

- *Dating Trait #3: He wants the real you*

So often women feel the need to sacrifice some part of themselves in order to make a relationship work. In the right relationship, there's no need. You don't have to hide, tone down, or apologize for any aspect of you or your fabulous life. With the right partner, you're not only able to be yourself, but you're better able to be the best version of your most authentic self. No compromises needed.

- *Dating Trait #4: He's trustworthy*

A relationship without trust is doomed from the start, but a relationship with abundant trust is a fabulous foundation for real, lasting love! Built over time, trust is based on the simple belief system that your partner has your best interests at heart and will never intentionally hurt you (and vice versa). If and when you discover that Mr. Next is one hundred percent trustworthy, you'll have no trouble giving your heart to him. In return, he'll most likely give you his heart and pave the way for a lasting, loving relationship to unfold.

- *Dating Trait #5: He enriches your life*

In the wrong relationship, your partner tears you to emotional shreds, brings you down, and in general, drains your energy. In the right relationship, he enriches your life, inspires you to be your best self, and brings a sense of peace and possibility to you. You'll know Mr. Next is enriching your life if and when he encourages and supports you professionally, personally, and spiritually. And when he does, he may just be Mr. Right!

Does your Mr. Next possess all five qualities? If so, congratulations! You have done your homework, chosen wisely, and are now well positioned for relationship success.

If not, pick yourself up, dust yourself off, and continue to seek God first in your decision making. Your relationship should bring glory to God, you, and your mate. Don't choose someone out of fear of loneliness or never getting married. You'd rather be alone than spend an eternity with someone who makes you miserable.

Chapter 8:
Wait a Minute; It Ain't Over
When it's all out of your system, here he comes again!

Just when I wasn't thinking about him any longer and was effectively healing from the saga of our ended relationship, enjoying my own little Gwendolyn's world as I call it, here he comes. He knows how I love Facebook, so that's the avenue he chose to keep a lookout on me and send messages. I should have never responded to him. Bad move on my part. Since I did respond, it opened the door for him to annoy the hell out of me, stir up old feelings, and get under my skin. Yet, anything you allow is permission to continue. So, here is what transpired via Facebook messages over a few months time before I truly had forgiven him.

Bishop: Hey, I heard you were dating. I see you rebounded quickly. You should be ashamed of yourself, woman of God. Tell whoever he is that he got a jewel when he got you. I never shall forget.

Gwendolyn: Well, I wonder how you could have possibly heard that. It's not even true. Must be gossip or you trying to figure out if I am or not. Anyway, I'm blessed, and thank you for releasing me. It has been a tremendous blessing. You be blessed and take care.

Bishop: I'm still hurting from our breakup. I'm trying to be strong. I know God will see me through this, but the pain is still present. Just keep me lifted in prayer as I continue to do his will. When I reach the place you are, I will send you a Facebook friend request. Love, Bishop.

Gwendolyn: LOL! LOL! LOL! Dude, you are hilarious. You think I haven't been informed that you're getting married. You ain't hurt at all. From one woman to the next, please. You're a womanizer. That's game you're writing. I know the devil's tricks when I see them, and you're clearly letting the devil use you. I'm laughing at the devil right now big time. When people move on, he shows up and tries to stir up something. Anyway, peace be unto you and grow up!

Bishop: Wow, I'm surprised by your cold response. You act like I am not supposed to have an emotional response to the death of our relationship. Many people have had to counsel me so that I could try to put the pieces back together. I cared for you when you were with your ex, then I asked you to be with me when that relationship ended. I have missed you and your daughters tremendously, and what we had. I begged you to stay in my life as a friend, but you refused and ended all communication with me. You act like I have no feelings. Maybe it meant nothing to you, but it did to me. I'm a Christian and you are my sister in Christ. This is not the way we are supposed to be. Where is the fruit of the spirit love, gentleness, meekness, goodness, temperance? Remember, when you stand praying for forgiveness, also forgive us our debts as we forgive our debtors. I'm reaching out to you. God is love and I still love you.

Now this particular message I didn't respond to. Immediately, my first thoughts were it was a load of crap. What is his problem that he wants women to lose their minds over him? I mean, he gets off by having women crying, begging, and hurting over him. I know personally it arouses him. All the time we were together, no matter how many kisses, touches, rubs, or whatever we did, he never had an erection, but the day after we split up and I'm crying and begging this idiot to be with me in a store parking lot, his little penis got hard as a rock. What the heck! My pain arouses him? That's sickening!

He had already disclosed to me that he met a prophetess on Noel Jones' dating website and started dating her two days after ending our relationship. He told me this during our meeting in the park. I believe he may have been talking to her over the internet a while. I don't believe two days after calling it quits with me, he discovered her. My name is Gwendolyn, not Lamont. I won't be the big dummy by believing that one bit. At the time he was sending me these messages, he was about two months into the relationship and engaged to be married to her. Plus, he got rid of me. So how in the world could he be hurting when our relationship was murdered by him and for all the wrong reasons? I didn't believe a word he said about him being hurt.

Now on the part regarding forgiveness, he was right. At that point, I was very hurt and even more hurt that he was dating and engaged to be married. He bragged about it over the pulpit and all over the internet. If I had responded to this message, I know I would have literally gone off. But, it didn't stop there.

Some time passed before we communicated again. Right before Christmas, he sent me a Merry Christmas message, and around this time, my family was dealing with two very tragic deaths. His message was titled *I Miss You*. He said he was listening to his recorder that I bought for him, when he heard my voice, which sounded so nice, and decided to send a hello and a Merry Christmas to me and the girls. I thanked him and let him know my family was going through some tremendous ordeals. He replied with kind words for me and my family and told me if I needed anything, he was one call away.

At the time, I was very vulnerable, so I did not reply because I didn't want to risk falling back in love with a man of words and no actions. Also, remember he was seeing a prophetess while he was sending me messages, and they were supposed to marry around Valentine's Day. However, I got a call that his Facebook relationship status changed once again back to single. I thought to myself that he was making himself look bad as a pastor. Every few months, he was in and out of a relationship according to what he posted on Facebook. When you're leading ministry, it definitely does not look good.

Then guess who sends me a friend request? The prophetess. When I accepted the request, I sent her a message saying I hoped he didn't do to her what he did to me. In response, she wrote on my Facebook wall saying she hoped I was healed from my relationship with him, and that he couldn't hurt her like he did me even if he wanted to because she wouldn't allow him. So, I sent her the following private message:

Well, prophetess, certainly I am healed and delivered from it. At one point, I was very angry, mad, and all that, but why be that way when I know what a powerful woman of God I am? So, I forgave him, not for him but for me, because surely forgiveness sets a person free. I also realized that hurt people hurt other people. He has some demons he has to face. It's apparent he gets a kick out of using women. I have messages in my inbox from him while he was dating you. I will never understand that man, and you know what? It's not for me to understand. It's for me to pray for him. Now I won't tell you that what he did to me didn't affect me, because it surely did. I was hurt a long time and so were my children. It hurts when someone brings you before their church and comes before your church family to discuss marriage, then suddenly dumps you with the only reason being "you're not in ministry & you don't have the finances to be married to a bishop" (which he is not a bishop over anything). That foolish behavior hurt. To you, prophetess, I apologize for coming at you wrong. When he told me the two of you were together, I was angry with him, and that's where my anger should have stayed. But, I am free from it and thankful I went through it. It has made me stronger.

The prophetess responded:

I praise God for you, your healing, and deliverance. I do forgive you, and I understand you were hurt by him. Because of who I am in God, I am able to see behind someone's demonic spirits & when I saw them in him, I immediately put a stop to the devil and any connection I had with him. He finally met someone that he couldn't control and manipulate. Don't get me wrong. He bought me the finest of everything, but at the end of the day, because of my ministry, I have to be married to someone who has integrity, is truly saved, and complements in ministry. He can't fill this role. Let's just say everything he told you that you weren't, he isn't either in no shape, form, or fashion. That's why I called the relationship and wedding off. I am glad you got to your next level. Keep pushing into your destiny, woman of God. I am here if you need me.

I thanked her for her reply and told her to have a Happy New Year.

So the Bishop was single again. I couldn't help but to laugh. It's true that what you put out comes back to you. A few days later, here he comes on Facebook again with a few messages. One saying *I miss you and Happy New Year*, and the second message saying *Sometimes the grass isn't greener on the other side.*

The third message was meant to be deep, I guess. *Singers put on choir robes, and ministers wear clergy collars each week and try to minister on the behalf of God. But, underneath every robe and every collar is a human being who is flawed but still called. The anointing will always be greater than the person with it. This is why so many talented people fall, because character and gifts don't grow up together. Gifts come without repentance. As a matter of fact, the bible does not say we're qualified. It says we're justified. We may not be qualified to man, but we're justified by God. God knows our hearts. You're a great woman, and not a day goes by that I don't think of you. I always want you to have the best.*

I understood what he was saying totally. I took it as an apology without him literally saying sorry. I do believe he is anointed, but his character doesn't line up with his gift.

I thanked him for his words, and a few days later, I saw him ride past my parents' house. Then he sent me another message saying he saw me, but I didn't reply to that one.

One day, I decided to be nosy and look at his Facebook wall. Again, he was talking to another woman, and the lady Sharon that I had a problem with in the beginning was back on the scene…the continuous circle of women and mindset of the bishop. Which one can he use and manipulate before he would move on to the next one?

I noticed one day the prophetess had deleted me as her friend on Facebook. I wondered why she had done that since we never spoke online after that initial discussion. I then received a phone call telling me that him and the prophetess had rekindled things and were scheduled to marry, yet two weeks before the wedding the prophetess' pastor informed her that if she was to marry this man, he would hinder her ministry. Again, she called off the wedding and the relationship. But, wait a minute. It still ain't over. The bishop then reaches out to my former pastor via Facebook, saying, *I think Gwendolyn needs closure. I would like to set up a meeting with you and her. I believe she needs closure.*

The pastor then called me up saying he received a message from a bishop, who he had no clue of who he was, regarding our breakup. I informed the pastor of who he was, but before then, I never informed the pastor about him. So, he actually made himself look stupid reaching out to someone who didn't have any idea as to who he is. I guess he thought I sat up running my mouth about him to various people, but I didn't. I had to get Gwendolyn back on track.

By this time, I was no longer concerned about him. So, I told my former pastor that I did not want to have a meeting with this man and that he was a manipulator. I had forgiven him as I was supposed to. The pastor informed him that I did not want a meeting. He then decided to tell the pastor his rendition of what happened to our relationship, trying to make himself appear to be more than what he truly was. Normally, people take this approach to cover up their true identity. Why try to justify your behavior or your decision to end a relationship if everything was done in decency and in order? Got Guilt?

Some bishop, huh? WHEN A MAN OF GOD HURTS YOU!

Chapter 9: Prayer

It truly does change things.

"Prayer changes things" is a common quote, but it certainly reigns true. I can't tell you the words to pray. Prayer is learned simply by praying. Prayer is intimate communication with God. My uncle has a saying that goes, "Prayer is simply taking everything you know about yourself — the good, the bad, the ugly, the downright nasty— and offering it up before everything you know about God." When he said this profound statement, all I could say is, "WOW!"

Then I thought about all that I was dealing with and took the time to pray. I even created a prayer schedule for myself. I set alarms in my phone for three different times of the day to take the time to pray and praise God. Sometimes we let our lives get too busy and forget some things. So, that was one reason I set the alarms. The other reason was because I feel like God loves his baby girl so much that he knows what time to expect me. I still have this schedule today to always pray and praise God.

I didn't have a deep tongue speaking prayer, but however you flow is quite alright. I would just tell God, "I'm hurting. I need you to come see about me." It would be simple prayers like that. I know when you're hurting it's hard to pray. You don't understand and may even think God has forgotten about you since he allowed you to go through it. I had to stay in prayer even in my pain for myself and him. Steve Harvey has a saying that goes, *Don't stop praying. It really does change things and people, too.*

Prayer is a beneficial part of your life, period, but when you are going through something, it is even more important to tell the Father how you're feeling. Sometimes when we go through trials and tribulations, we get caught up in it and stop praying and acknowledging God. Surely, if He brought you to it, He will bring you through it. The idle mind is the devil's playground, and the enemy can creep in on people who are hurting and depressed.

Just talk to God. Imagine meeting your best friend for coffee at your favorite café. Your friend knows everything about you. You can count on your friend being exactly where he says he will be. Anytime you need him, you can call and he won't be upset with you. He is willing to listen and responds with love and concern.

That is just like prayer. The only difference is that your best friend is God. God is available to you 24 hours a day, 7 days a week. He knows everything you ever did, and He still loves you! He knows your future, too. He has the best plans for your life. He cares for you so much that He gave His Son so that you could be with Him forever. "For God so loved the world that He gave His one and only Son, that whosoever believes in Him shall not perish, but have eternal life," (John 3:16). You can talk to Him about anything that concerns you. Tell Him your desires and passions. Share your concerns for your loved ones. Talk out your fears with Him. Communicate to God what is inside you without fear.

Prayer – What do I say?

Prayer may be accomplished in many ways. The best way is to be natural, just as if you were in the room with Him. He is very anxious to hear every word you say. You can say whatever is on your heart. He'll even listen to your anger and sadness.

In Matthew 6:9-13, Jesus taught the disciples a pattern for prayer. "This, then, is how you should pray: 'Our Father in heaven, hallowed be your name, your kingdom come, your will be done on earth as it is in heaven. Give us today our daily bread. Forgive us our debts, as we also have forgiven our debtors. And lead us not into temptation, but deliver us from the evil one.'"

Prayer – Why Pray?

Why is prayer important? If God already knows all about you and knows all that He has written, why should you pray? It's because God created us to have free will. He wants us to come to Him willingly and not as robotic creations. He has given us a mind to make decisions, and the most important decision is about eternity. Even though He knows the future, we don't know the future choices we will make. It's important to live by His guidance to make the right choices.

In the Bible, you will find that kings, prophets, and ordinary people like you and me averted destruction by praying to God. One prayer stopped the sun, one prayed fire down from heaven, one gained fifteen years to his own life, and one prayer even saved a whole city. These people prayed intensely to the God who answers prayer. When you pray, God listens to your cries. When you don't pray, God feels left out of your life.

"He is patient with you, not wanting anyone to perish, but everyone to come to repentance," (2 Peter 3:9). As you pray consistently, you are affirming the existence of God in your life. You are building your faith as you see God's hand do His mighty work on your behalf just because you asked.

Chapter 10:
It's All About You!!!

The shocking truth about you! Self-examination time!

When you sit down and truly analyze yourself, sometimes the reality of who you really are may shock you. But, until you accept the reality of you, the false image you may have of yourself is just that: a fake and phony. You can't be anything to anybody else until you address the issues within yourself.

I had to look in the mirror and see myself for who I really am. I didn't go on what others think of me and neither should you. I almost let the negative things people have said to me or about me become me. Have you let other people paint a picture of what you should be based on what they want you to be? Don't! Give them back their brushes and let God paint the picture of you. No matter what people say, face it, you will never amount up to what man wants you to be, but does that matter? NO! God matters. Know who you are, what you are, and whose you are in Christ Jesus!

Analyze yourself and the truth about you. No one knows you like you. There were some things about me that I disliked, hated, and were ashamed of. I disliked the fact that, in my twenties, I never really gave the men that I dated a fair chance. I was selfish and only concerned about me. I didn't like the fact that I moved quickly from one mate to the next, and I surely hated some of the things I had done before my children. I didn't like a lot of my behaviors, things I had done and said about other people. I didn't like myself. This was an honest and true self-analysis for me, and it brought me to tears.

However, when I did analyze the person I truly am, I was able to address it and start making a list of things that needed to be transformed…not changed, but transformed. When you change from a thing, it's possible to change back to that particular thing. But, like the cartoon *The Transformers*, when you're transformed, it's into something totally different that you couldn't recognize before.

So, I began to transform my life by letting go of some people and habits no matter who and what they were. I had to get myself on track. I can't continuously go through life making others pay for my insecurities or possibly my daughters reaping the harvest from the shameful seeds in life that I planted from the lifestyle I once led. I even stopped frequenting certain places and doing plenty of things in my life. This was not easy. It hurt, but it needed to happen. Sometimes in your life there will come a time when you have to walk alone. The word of God teaches us in Romans 12:2, "Be not conformed to this word, but be ye transformed by the renewing of your mind, that ye may prove what is good and acceptable and the perfect will of God."

Get to know all you can about yourself. There is no "I can't" in life. You can be whoever you want to be. The key is to never give up, and even if you fail at what you aspire to do, keep trying. All successful people have some failures behind them.

Do you know how beautiful you are within? Outer appearance is one thing, but do you know the beauty within you? When I analyzed myself underneath the joyous smile and vibrant personality everyone loves, I could go down the list of things I had to address about myself. When we can take the time to do this, it will help you further down the road.

Low Self-Esteem

Many people deal with low self-esteem issues. This isn't a woman or man thing. People in general can encounter issues of low self-esteem. Growing up, I was teased a lot and called skinny, ugly, and poor, among other things. So, with my self-esteem being low, I would find myself in the arms of whoever made me feel good about myself. Some I knew I had no business being with, like married men. As I said, I had to analyze myself. I was someone I didn't like.

Ask yourself what do you like about yourself? Are you proud of yourself? Do you love, honor, and respect yourself? Self-esteem comes from the inside out. It means you are not depending on anyone else to validate you or make you feel good about yourself because you already know you're fine with still working on a better you. You're confident and aware of your strength and abilities.

Self-esteem is a core identity issue essential to personal validation and our ability to experience joy. Once it's achieved, it comes from the inside out. A person with low self-esteem does not feel good about themselves because they have absorbed negative messages from their culture and/or relationships. Maybe people in their family, school, work, or even neighbors have said and done things that make them feel worthless. Poor self-esteem often results in depression and anxiety. Physical health suffers, as well.

You can choose your identity. For some women, it's hard, but I challenge you. See yourself the way God sees you. 1 Cor. 13:12 - *For now, we see through a glass darkly; but then face to face. Now I know in part; but then shall I know even as also I am known.* You are

His creation, His masterpiece, one of His designer's original. You are truly beautiful. Who can be the best you besides you? Don't try and be anybody's second best. Be your first best. Change the perception of you. When you change the way you see yourself, it will change your reputation and your attitude. Believe in yourself.

<u>Attitude</u>

According to the dictionary, the word attitude means an internal position or feeling with regard to something else. Other words often used as synonyms are: disposition, feeling, mood, opinion, sentiment, temper, etc. Now I'm not stereotyping women, but the number one complaint I hear from men, supervisors, pastors, children, etc. is about attitudes. I know there have been times when I have given people much "tude", and for what? Having a bad attitude does more harm than good.

That woman and her attitude! Ladies, I know we have times when we get upset, mad, or what have you. All humans let their emotions take over sometimes. But what's with the sudden attitude? The sun comes up and you're being nasty to others who have clearly not done anything to you. Then by the time lunch hour rolls around, you're all smiles and laughter, and by dinnertime, here comes the "tude" again. Are you bi-polar? Some would think so.

When I would have my "tude", since I'm not one for verbal confrontation, I would do the whole isolation thing. You wouldn't hear from me nor see me. I'm still dealing with overcoming this. When things bother me or I don't want to be bothered, I cut all ties with a person. Sometimes we'll rekindle, and other times we won't. I need to just start opening my mouth and letting people know how I truly feel and why I want nothing to do with them. I know better about this behavior now, especially with being in my thirties. I can sit down and have logical-non emotional discussions with people. Come out of the emotions and put the issues on the table.

We seriously need to check our attitudes. What man wants a woman who switches on him constantly? Some men are afraid to approach us because of this very reason. Most of us can easily identify a bad attitude when they are displayed outwardly or actions such as negativity, criticalness, rebellion, defiance, impatience, uncooperative, apathy, discouragement, independence, presumption, arrogance, self-centeredness, rudeness, and such. These are examples which we should reject, especially as Christians.

However, keep in mind attitudes are inner dispositions of the heart and thoughts. They are hidden intentions which will eventually serve as the basis for our actions. "For as a man thinketh in his heart, so is he," (Proverbs 23:7). In reality, no one else really knows the thoughts of your heart except you and God. Consequently, attitude is something that only you and God can work out. A change must take place inwardly. They say attitude determines altitude, and I believe that wholeheartedly. A pleasant attitude can go a lot further than a bad one.

Get To Know Yourself

You're a very interesting person! Who are you? What do you stand for? What do you believe in? What engages your passion? What brings tears of gratitude and joy to your eyes?

When I began dating the bishop, in all I did I made sure I had time for him. I would leave my church doing ninety mph to get to his. If he called, I answered on the first ring. When I was with him, I focused solely on him and really tried to get to know him. Now what if I had taken that same approach with rediscovering myself? So, I took baby steps toward getting reacquainted with myself. Hopefully some things I did will help you.

Spend time with yourself. You can uncover great things about yourself during "ME" time. Who you are, whose you are, where you are, where you're trying to go, who you're becoming, and what you are capable of. It's all part of accepting the reality of you.

Keep a journal. Writing your thoughts on paper can be profound. I shock myself at some of the things I write. Get yourself a nice notebook and go for it. Don't worry about making sure the grammar is correct. Just write. It makes you feel free. Even write down scriptures or quotes, and meditate on them. Read, as well. I have created a new collection of books for myself. Always read. You should never stop feeding your mind.

Meditate. Meditation is not about attaining a state of emptiness while sitting in the lotus position. It's about observing yourself in the present moment. Your goal should be to empty yourself of any anxiety or worry. Acknowledge them, but don't focus on understanding what they mean or solve any problems. Just allow yourself to be still and relax.

Walk or Drive. Sometimes it may be good to just get out of your home. Walking is good for your body. It's moving meditation. It allows you to notice what's going on around you and appreciate the world you live in. If you're like me and always moving a million miles per hour, walking can allow you to focus on being fully present, while indulging in the movement you find so vital. It can provide you with an opportunity to mull over something that may be on your mind. Driving also can prove to be an interesting process, especially if it's difficult to find a quiet place in your home. Pop your favorite CD in and hit the road. See where your "self" leads you.

Take yourself out. A day spent wandering the mall, a few hours spent in a store, taking in an afternoon matinee, eating at your favorite restaurant, reading in a coffee shop, being pampered in a spa. These are some authentic outings, and indulging in activities like these is similar to dating yourself. Just take time to be with you with no other purpose than sheer enjoyment.

Nuggets for the Ladies

- If you're being abused (abnormally used) in any way physical, verbal, emotionally...GET HELP NOW!
- If you're not ready for a serious relationship or marriage, don't play with him. Don't mess his life up with your immaturity.
- He who findeth a wife findeth a good thing and obtain favor from the Lord. Are you qualified to be a wife?
- You can't be the boss, and if you're going to lead, why'd you marry him? The reason he won't commit is because you probably won't submit. A real man isn't going to let

his family down. So stop all the nagging. *Proverbs 27:15-16*

- Y'all don't like this word...SUBMIT. If you married him, SUBMIT. He is the leader. Let him lead and be his helpmeet. Help him meet the needs.
- YOU WERE CREATED IN HIS IMAGE AND LIKENESS. ANOTHER PERSON CANNOT COMPLETE YOU. DISCOVER THE REAL YOU AND KNOW YOUR WORTH!
- Contrary to popular belief, THERE ARE STILL SOME GOOD MEN OUT THERE! Question is are you good enough for them? Hmmm…
- Wouldn't it be refreshing to listen to him talk to you about his dreams, goals, and his spiritual walk. Find out what's in his heart!
- Contrary to popular belief, the best way to get over one man IS NOT to get under a new one. Get yourself together before you can be anything to anyone else.
- Take some time from dude to dude. If you still have the scent of your ex on you trying to mix with his scent and yours…I BET IT STINKS! Get one out of your system before you move on to the next.
- Matter of fact, he ain't the ex, so don't hold him accountable for what the last man did. If you keep

comparing him to your ex, he is going to find his next.
- And if you're going to compare him to the ex, that's who you need to be with. Enough said!
- What's with the attitudes? Sometimes, you're sweet as pie, and other times, you're a demon. Lose the BAD 'TUDE IF YOU WANNA KEEP YOUR DUDE.

Sex

Yes, let's talk about sex. I remember hearing a song by Trin-i-Tee 5:7, and some of the lyrics went:

> *Who do you think I am; I don't play these games*
> *Not goin' out like that; let me explain*
> *Tryin' to save myself; don't pressure me*
> *My spirit leads me to celibacy*
> *I have to just be real and I know it's fair*
> *I wanna please my God and I don't care*
> *You can just leave now, but if you stay*
> *There's gonna be no other way*

The lyrics simply are telling us if he is not your husband, he does not deserve your body. Back in the day, that's what I used - my body, not taking the time to really know people. I just thought men were looking for a good time in bed. Now I think back over the many years, and I feel convicted, truly convicted. When you're freely sharing your body with someone who is not your husband, you are disrespecting God.

How can I open my mouth and say I love God, but love the way this man feels on top of me more? No way! God doesn't play games like that. Your body is His temple. While single, devote your life to God and your body. I know it feels good to you, but it doesn't mean it's good for you. If a man cannot be in your life without you backing it up, dropping it like it's hot, going down on him, tea bagging, having a threesome, and all of that nonsense, he doesn't need to be in your life. A real man respects God, himself, and you, and he will not let you lay with him before taking a covenant before God.

Close your legs, ladies. I know this is not easy. Trust, it wasn't for me. Men were so used to the old ways of Gwendolyn that when I started talking about God and celibacy, they found themselves another chick. But, there will be one who knows what to say and how to say it. That's when you're going to need some super strength not to give in to him. Ladies, y'all know the one who makes you feel like a queen with words but no action besides the bedroom. Even in the bedroom he makes you feel like his penis is anointed because of the way he makes your body feel. Yep, him, ladies. Flee from him. Let God penetrate you. Become intimate with the Father. He can give the greatest climax ever!

Tongue

Proverbs 18:21: "Death and life are in the power of the tongue, and they that love it shall eat the fruit thereof." Now surely we know our mouths are lethal weapons and can get us into a world of trouble. You don't have to have the last word all the time. Everyone really doesn't need a piece of your mind. Quite frankly, sometimes we as women just need to know when to SHUT UP!

Words can build up and also tear down. Watch what you say, how you say it, when you say it, and to whom you say it. If you're one of those emotional people that break down when something is said to you that you don't like or agree with, then your sensitive, emotional self should be the first to keep your mouth closed.

I know I have said one too many things that can be the determining factor whether a relationship lasts or ends. Even in relationships with others, we always have to be mindful of what we say and how we say it. Think before you speak. Think about how you would feel if it were being said to you. If you get a negative feeling about it, then by all means don't speak it. We have the power to speak life into others, as well as death. So, ladies, sometimes you just need to let your bottom lip meet your top lip and SHUT UP!

Purity

According to the dictionary, purity is the absence of impurity in a substance or abstinence from vices and/or abundance of virtue. In the process of me working on this book, my former church home had a wonderful women's retreat, and the main topic was purity. God laid it on the pastor's heart for the women's ministry. Most people may think purity for a woman means celibacy, but the pastor and Prophet Wilson helped me to realize it's more than that.

As a woman of God, surely abstaining from sex is something we all should do. However, don't stop there. Purity is not just about keeping your legs, mouth, and any other body part closed. It's about being pure in heart, mind, and soul. Your conversations, your thoughts, and even your heart are pure.

We took that weekend to come together and rededicate ourselves to Christ. During that weekend, not only did I let some things go, but some of the other sisters did, as well. It was so much stuff that I could discuss with my sisters. Yet, I was still holding on to some things. It was time to let go and give it over to God.

Take some time to reflect and pray about yourself and anything you may be dealing with or think you may be holding on to that needs to come up and out. After this ordeal with this man and other things in my life, there was simply no one that could comfort me like Jesus. All the teary-eyed nights and the lonely days, Jesus pulled me through it all. I owe Him my praise, my worship, reading His word, and telling others about Him. We all mess up from time to time, and simply don't understand what's going on in the world around us. Don't give up on God. Trust Him and rededicate yourself to Him.

After rediscovering you and rededicating yourself back to God, when hurt arises in any form, identify it, acknowledge it, pray, forgive, and release it to God. Don't carry these burdens in your heart. After that man of God hurt me, I thought I would never love again. In fact, I didn't even want to. But, that's not what God designed me for. So, I am free to love and live again!

Remember this: everything that started, it was started by God...even you. Many books or statements tell us to find our inner selves. That's all fine and dandy, but the truth of the matter is, you need to find your way back to God. He is your purpose, your reason for living. He created you. It all begins with Him, so return to Him. I returned to Him solely, and He began to restore me back to a place in Him. Pray, praise, worship, study the word of God, and fellowship with other believers. Alright...Ready, Set, Go!

A Final Word from the Author

Now that you have read this book thoroughly, I hope you feel empowered to reestablish your life the way God would want it. There will be times of hurt, trials, and tribulations. No one is exempt from it. 1 Peter 5: 10 - *But the God of all grace, who hath called us unto his eternal glory by Christ Jesus, after that ye have suffered a while, make you perfect, establish, strengthen, and settle you.* Yet, it's not easy to pick yourself up, dust yourself off, and get back in the game of life. This book was not written to condemn, but it's centered solely on overcoming. Say it with me: YOU HAVE THE POWER TO OVERCOME.

So many people deal with this type of hurt, and there needed to be something said and wisdom given to overcome. Warning comes before destruction, and I had plenty of warnings that went ignored because I was caught up in my emotions. Even the strongest, most Bible versed, demon-casting-out, speaking-in-tongue folks can get caught off guard. We must also realize there are some people who are anointed to see vulnerability and they prey on it. Once you let them in, they mess you up even more. Be mindful of who you let in your circle, especially if they can always critique you but never assist you.

Woman or Man who has taken the time to read this, my sincere prayer is that you feel that you're taking back the steering wheel to your life with God as your navigational system. I hope you can get back to the place where God wants you and can use you effectively. Your confidence has been returned to you, your hope returned to you, your joy restored, and most of all, your love for yourself and your faith in God renewed! He won't leave you nor forsake you at any time in your life. I hope you have read something that has helped you, and sharing this testimony lets you know no one is alone when dealing with these types of situations.

Ode to Love

I was walking down the street one day and I met love.
Love greeted me and we talked for a while.
Love and I became good friends.
We learned a lot about one another.
I enjoyed love, so I took it everywhere I went.
Love was beautiful.
Everyone complimented me on love.
I went to bed every night with love on my mind.
One morning, I arose to find that love was gone.
Love moved on to the next victim.
I still ached from the arrow I had been hit with.
Love held me hostage and I liked it.
When love told me what to do, I asked no questions.
I obliged it.
When love called, I answered it; now it's gone.
Love taught many lessons that I will never forget.
Now love has set me free to love again

To order additional copies of this book or to contact the author, please visit www.merilynwilliams.com

Connect with her on Facebook at www.facebook.com/restoredmerl

Follow her on Twitter at www.twitter.com/authormerl

Stay tuned for the upcoming novel from Merilyn Williams:

Ain't No Hurt Like Church Hurt

& More!